# GARLAND STUDIES
# IN ENTREPRENEURSHIP

*edited by*

**STUART BRUCHEY**
UNIVERSITY OF MAINE

A GARLAND SERIES

**DATE DUE**

| | | | |
|---|---|---|---|
| | | | |
| | | | |
| | | | |
| | | | |
| | | | |
| | | | |
| | | | |
| | | | |
| | | | |
| | | | |
| | | | |
| | | | |
| | | | |
| | | | |
| | | | |
| | | | |
| | | | |

# ACCOUNTING AND AUDITING OF SMALL BUSINESSES

JOE GREGORY BUSHONG

GARLAND PUBLISHING, INC.
NEW YORK & LONDON / 1995

**Library of Congress Cataloging-in-Publication Data**

Bushong, Joe Gregory.
    Accounting and auditing of small businesses / Joe Gregory Bushong.
      p.   cm. — (Garland studies in entrepreneurship)
    Includes bibliographical references (p. ) and index.
    ISBN 0–8153–1935–5 (alk. paper)
    1. Financial statements—Standards—United States.  2. Small busi-
ness—United States—Accounting.  3. Small business—United States—
Auditing.   I. Title.  II. Series.
HF5681.B2B87  1995
657'.9042—dc20                                94–32962
                                                    CIP

Printed on acid-free, 250-year-life paper
Manufactured in the United States of America

# CONTENTS

*Contents*

# Accounting and Auditing
# of Small Businesses

# I
# INTRODUCTION

Accounting standards overload has received considerable attention by the accounting profession during the last several years. Accounting standards overload has resulted from standards becoming more numerous, more complex, and more specific. The problem is compounded by failure to provide for differences in private and public entities and large and small enterprises (AICPA 1981, 4). In the twenty-one years the Financial Accounting Standards Board (FASB) has been in existence, it has issued 117 Statements of Financial Accounting Standards. The FASB's two predecessor bodies, the Committee on Accounting Procedure and the Accounting Principles Board, issued a total of eighty-two standards in their combined existence of thirty-four years.

The problem of accounting standards overload is particularly acute for small and/or privately held businesses. Small privately owned businesses are subject to the same Generally Accepted Accounting Principles (GAAP) as large publicly held businesses[1] (AICPA 1981, 5). However, there is a perception that financial statements prepared in conformance with GAAP for small and/or privately held businesses may not provide useful information and may be inordinately costly to prepare.

The accounting profession has devoted considerable attention to this problem over the last several years. Since 1976 the American Institute of Certified Public Accountants (AICPA) has had three separate committees address the issue[2], and the FASB has issued a special report on the subject (FASB 1983) in addition to sponsoring a major research study in conjunction with the National Association of Accountants (Abdel-khalik et al. 1983). Several studies have also been performed by individuals and groups.[3] The current practice of the

FASB is to consider the small business aspects of all issues that the FASB addresses. However, little relief has been provided to small businesses from the problem of accounting standards overload.

## THE IMPORTANCE OF SMALL BUSINESS IN THE ECONOMY

Estimates of the number of small businesses and their contribution to the nation's economy vary. One source of information is the Internal Revenue Service's *Statistics of Income Bulletin* (IRS 1987). For 1984, the last year for which complete information is reported, approximately 16.1 million non-farm business returns were filed. The total included corporation returns (3.2 million), partnership returns (1.6 million), and proprietorship returns (11.3 million). Of the total returns filed, 12.6 million (78%) showed total gross receipts of less than $100,000 (IRS 1987, 83). According to Small Business Administration statistics, firms with less than 100 employees comprised 97.2% of all business establishments during 1984 (SBA 1986, 11).

Not only do small businesses make up the overwhelming majority of the number of businesses in the United States, they also make a substantial contribution to employment. In 1984, businesses with less than 100 employees employed 50.4% of all workers (SBA 1986, 11). In the period December 1984 to December 1985, employment in the U.S. grew by 2 million. Growth in employment in small-business-dominated industries (5.1%) was greater than growth in large-business-dominated industries (.7%) (SBA 1986, 6). During the period 1979 to 1983, a period which saw a sharp rise in the unemployment rate, small businesses created most of the net new jobs, and wage and salary jobs grew faster in small businesses than in large businesses (SBA 1986, 225). The 1980-1986 period saw 10.5 million new jobs created in the United States. Businesses with less than 100 employees created 63.5% of these new jobs, and businesses with less than twenty employees created 38.7% (SBA 1988). This employment growth in the small-businesses-dominated sectors of the economy continues. Frank Swain, Chief Counsel for Advocacy for the Small Business Administration, reports that in 1986 small-business-dominated industries increased employment at a rate 74% higher than the national average and eight times higher than the remainder of the economy (Swain 1987, 112).

Although small businesses are an important and growing sector of the economy, GAAP are designed for users of the financial statements of large public entities (AICPA 1981, 11). The needs of the large number of businesses at the small end of the size spectrum are often overlooked when accounting standards are established (AICPA 1983, 2). This has led to the concerns that small companies are required to provide financial information that is not needed by the users of their financial statements, and that the required information is often costly to prepare and precludes the companies from providing other more useful information (FASB 1981, 1).

*Statement of Financial Accounting Concepts No. 1* states: "The information provided by financial reporting involves a cost to provide and use and generally the benefits of information provided should be expected to at least equal the cost involved." (FASB 1978b, par. 23) The concern that the cost of providing financial statements for small businesses in conformance with GAAP outweighs the benefits derived has been the subject of considerable research. Several of these studies are summarized in the next section of this paper and are discussed in detail in a later chapter.

## PRIOR RESEARCH

Prior research has addressed the question of whether financial statements prepared on a basis other than GAAP are as useful or more useful than financial statements prepared in conformance with GAAP. Bankers have been identified as the primary external users of small business financial statements (AICPA 1976, 10; Abdel-khalik et al. 1983, 1; and FASB 1983, 3). Much of the research used bankers as respondents or subjects, although other groups such as managers of small businesses and CPAs who service small business clients have been included as respondents. Because of conflicting findings, the research has not conclusively answered the question concerning the usefulness to bankers of non-GAAP financial statements for small businesses.

Two studies have been conducted by or for the Financial Accounting Standards Board. In 1981 the FASB issued an *Invitation to Comment, Financial Reporting by Private and Small Public Companies* (FASB 1981). Responses were received from CPAs, managers, and external users of small company financial statements. A majority (80%) of the external users responding to the invitation to comment were bankers.

A large majority (71%) of the bankers responded that they require the same financial information for their small clients as they require for their large clients. However, a majority (58%) of the bankers also responded that they are more interested in short-term cash flows than in accrual basis earnings. Forty-seven percent of the bankers responding to a question concerning whether small businesses could account for their activities differently than large companies without decreasing the usefulness of their financial statements felt they could. Forty-three percent felt they could not. The remaining 10% percent were not sure. Over 80% of the bankers reported satisfaction with the information in financial statements that are audited or reviewed, but only 50% reported satisfaction with the information in financial statements that are compiled.

A majority of the CPAs responding to the invitation to comment believe that users of small business financial statements do not have the same financial information needs as users of large business financial statements. A majority of the CPAs also believe that small businesses could account for their activities differently than large businesses without decreasing the usefulness of their financial statements.

Abdel-khalik et al. (1983) performed one of the more comprehensive studies concerning the problem of accounting for small businesses. The study was performed for the Financial Accounting Standards Board and was partially sponsored by the National Association of Accountants. Responses were obtained from bankers, CPAs, and upper level managers from small privately held companies.

A four-step approach to the research was used. For each of the three groups the researchers conducted exploratory interviews with a small sample. After the results of the exploratory interviews were analyzed, in-depth interviews were conducted with members of each of the three groups. These interviews were then followed by survey questionnaires for each of the three groups, and follow-up interviews were conducted for a sample of the banking and accounting respondents to the questionnaires. No hypotheses were tested.

Ninety percent of the responding bankers agreed that GAAP financial statements are more reliable for use by bankers and provide more understandable information than non-GAAP financial statements. However, the study also found that bankers equate GAAP financial statements with audited financial statements. During preliminary and follow-up interviews, the interviewers frequently had to explain the differences in statements prepared in conformance with GAAP and audited statements.

Although the bankers indicated that statements prepared in conformance with GAAP are preferred, they also indicated that often statements not in conformance with GAAP are accepted. Normally, when non-GAAP statements are accepted no action is taken against the borrower in the way of more restrictive covenants or increased interest rates.

The accountants in the survey also believed that statements prepared in conformance with GAAP are more reliable than statements prepared on some other basis. However, for some requirements, the CPA respondents do not follow GAAP for their small company clients as often as 70% of the time.

There were some notable differences in opinion between the bankers and the accountants. Of the banker respondents, 85% reported that the same information is needed from private and public companies for use in making similar decisions, and that financial statements will be less useful if an accounting basis other than GAAP is used. However, only 40% of the accountants agreed with those assertions. A larger percentage of accountants than bankers reported that external users place less reliance on the financial statements of private companies than on the financial statements of publicly held companies. The accountants also believe that external users can obtain information in addition to the financial statements more easily from private companies than from public companies.

Knutson and Wichmann (1984) tested whether CPAs perceive a difference in the importance of twenty-two different disclosure requirements for different sized companies (small, medium, and large) and different types of companies (publicly or privately held). The hypothesis of no difference in importance of disclosure requirements for companies of different sizes or types was rejected for all twenty-two disclosure requirements. The major conclusion of this study is that CPAs perceive a difference in the disclosure requirements of companies based on the size of the company (large or small) and the type (publicly or privately held).

Stanga and Tiller (1983) asked loan officers to indicate their needs for items of accounting information on a five-point scale from not important to very important. One group was asked to respond as if they were considering a significant loan to a large public industrial company, and the other group was asked to respond as if they were considering a significant loan to a small private industrial company. The mean rankings of the responses did not vary significantly from the large bank group to the small bank group. This suggests that bankers place the same value on information when considering a loan for a small company as when considering a loan for a large company. However, the results show that several items required to be reported by GAAP are not as important to either group as some information not currently reported. For example, both groups of bankers responded that forecast revenue, net income, capital expenditures, and planned financing are more important than many items required by GAAP, including capital lease information and deferred tax information.

Nair and Rittenberg (1983) surveyed small businessmen, certified public accountants, and small bankers in an effort to determine the needs of the users of small business financial statements. Their results were inconclusive concerning the needs of bankers. The bankers were evenly divided on whether they relied less on financial statements of small businesses than on financial statements of large businesses. The majority of bankers agreed that they are not as concerned with complexities created by GAAP when considering loans for small businesses as they are when considering loans for large businesses. However, they also agreed that there are no substantial differences in decisions made by users of small business financial statements than in decisions made by the users of large business financial statements.

Campbell (1984) used protocol analysis to examine bankers' use of four items of accounting information that are often considered not useful by bankers when evaluating potential loans for small businesses. Two subjects received financial statements prepared in conformance with GAAP. The other two subjects received financial statements with earnings per share, deferred income taxes, capitalized lease, and inflation-adjusted information excluded. The results indicate that the capitalized lease information was the only information item of the four tested that was used by the bankers in evaluating the proposed loan.

Benson (1985) used mail surveys and protocol analysis to evaluate the usefulness to bankers of twenty-nine items of accounting information that are required to be reported by GAAP. Of the twenty-nine items evaluated, six are perceived as not useful, sixteen intermediately useful, and seven as highly useful. Benson found that 59 % of the financial statements accepted by the bankers were prepared on a basis other than GAAP. The survey found that bankers have different information needs for small private companies than for large public companies. The bankers also believe that the financial statements of those companies are less useful than the statements of large public companies, and that differential measurement and differential disclosure should be permitted.

Hiltebeitel (1985) used an experiment with bankers as subjects to compare the usefulness of financial statements prepared in conformance with GAAP with financial statements prepared with various departures from GAAP. He also analyzed the effects of demographics on the bankers' responses. The four sets of statements used were: (1) prepared in conformance with GAAP, (2) prepared in conformance with GAAP but the statement of changes in financial position was not included, (3) included departures from GAAP for accounting for income taxes, accounting for leases, accounting for capitalization of interest, and presentation of the statement of changes in financial position, and (4) included the departures in (3) but the statement of changes in financial position was provided. The bankers perceived the financial statements that included all four departures from GAAP as statistically less useful than the other three sets of statements. However, those modifications did not affect the bankers' needs for additional information.

Williams (1987) used a quasi-experiment to examine perceptions of relevance and cost effectiveness of financial statements prepared in conformance with GAAP and financial statements prepared with some GAAP requirements omitted. Four GAAP requirements were examined: (1) accounting for leases, (2) capitalization of interest on construction, (3) accounting for deferred taxes, and (4) accounting for compensated absences. Responses were obtained from bankers, controllers, and auditors from local, regional, and national firms. Results indicated that the four accounting standards tend to be more relevant than cost effective. Bankers tended to view the standards as less relevant and less cost effective than the other two groups.

No consensus has been reached in the literature concerning the usefulness to bankers of financial statements prepared in conformance with GAAP for small businesses. When asked, bankers indicate they need the same financial information for their small private clients as they need for their large public clients (FASB 1983, Abdel-khalik et al. 1983, Stanga & Tiller 1983). However, other research does not support bankers' contentions that they need the same information for both groups of clients. These areas of differences are:

1. Bankers routinely accept financial statements that are not in conformance with GAAP. (FASB 1983, Abdel-khalik et al. 1983).

2. Empirical research has found that bankers do not use at least some of the information required by GAAP (Campbell 1984, Benson 1985, Hiltebeitel 1985).

3. Certified public accountants generally believe that small private businesses can account for their operations differently than large public companies without decreasing the usefulness of their financial statements (FASB 1983, Abdel-khalik et al. 1983, and Knutson and Wichmann 1984).

Because of these differences in the research results, small businesses have received little relief from the problem of accounting standards overload. There are several possible reasons for these reported differences. These are discussed in a later section of this chapter.

## MOTIVATION FOR THE STUDY

The detailed requirements of current GAAP are burdensome and costly for all businesses to apply. However, the problem is particularly acute for small/private businesses (AICPA 1981, 5). The evidence concerning whether small/private businesses can be allowed to account for their operations differently from large or public companies without decreasing the usefulness of those statements to bankers is inconclusive.

The objective of financial reporting is to provide information that is useful in decision making (FASB 1978b). If current GAAP requirements are more useful than a non-GAAP alternative, the use of statements prepared in conformance with GAAP should result in different decisions than if the statements were prepared using a non-GAAP alternative. The purpose of this study is to provide evidence concerning whether there are differences in the decisions of bank loan officers, the primary external users of small business financial statements (AICPA 1976, 10; Abdel-khalik et al. 1983, 1; and FASB

1983, 3), when they use financial statements prepared in conformance with GAAP compared to financial statements prepared using a non-GAAP alternative.

## FORMULATION OF THE RESEARCH QUESTION

The research question is based on and is an extension of the prior research. The prior research has provided conflicting results concerning whether bankers need financial statements prepared in conformance with GAAP for their small/private clients. There are several possible reasons for these conflicts. These reasons include:

1. Bankers require the same information for both small private and large public companies, but they do not require the same information as financial analysts. Although GAAP are intended to serve some of the information needs of all financial statement users, they are designed from the perspective of financial analysts and stockholders in public companies (AICPA 1976, 9-10). Research (Benjamin and Stanga 1977) has shown that bankers and financial analysts do not have the same financial information needs. When bankers report the same information needs for both small private and large public companies, it may not follow that they need financial statements prepared in conformance with GAAP.

2. Bankers perceive accounting information as being cost free to them. Therefore, when asked, they will respond that more rather than less information is required, but all the information may not be used in their loan-granting decision.

3. CPAs are more familiar with how small private companies differ from large public companies and with what accounting standards measure and how they were developed than are bankers. Therefore,

CPAs' perceptions of the reporting requirements of small private companies differ from the perceptions of bankers.

4. When bankers report that they require financial statements prepared in conformance with GAAP, what they actually require are financial statements that have been audited or reviewed. This is suggested in the research of both Abdel-khalik et al. (1983) and the FASB (1983).

None of the research to date has examined the possible causes of the conflicting findings. The research reported in this study was designed to examine the fourth possible reason for the conflicts found in the research, that is, the research examined the interaction between the type of accountants' report and the basis of accounting used in the financial statements. The primary research question is:

Does the type of accountants' report and the basis of accounting interact to affect a line of credit decision made by bank loan officers when evaluating a loan for a small private company?

Secondary research questions are:

1. Does the type of accountants' report affect a line of credit decision made by bank loan officers when evaluating a loan for a small private company?

2. Does the basis of accounting affect a line of credit decision made by bank loan officers when evaluating a loan for a small private company?

## METHODOLOGY

Bank loan officers have been identified as the primary external users of small business financial statements (AICPA 1976, 10; Abdel-khalik et al. 1983, 1; and FASB 1983, 3); therefore, the participants were bank loan officers.

The research design is a 3 X 2 factorial design. The independent variables are the accountants' report on the financial statements and the basis of accounting. The three levels of accountants' report are the audit report, the review report, and the compilation report. The two levels of basis of accounting are statements prepared in conformance with GAAP and statements prepared with some GAAP requirements omitted. The research design is shown in figure 1.

FIGURE 1
RESEARCH DESIGN

BASIS OF ACCOUNTING

|  |  | GAAP | MODIFIED GAAP |
|---|---|---|---|
| TYPE | AUDIT |  |  |
| OF | REVIEW |  |  |
| REPORT | COMPILATION |  |  |

The participants who received the GAAP basis statements received statements prepared in conformance with GAAP and the statements were accompanied by either an audit, review, or compilation report. The participants who received the modified GAAP statements received statements prepared in conformance with GAAP, but the measurement requirements of four accounting pronouncements (discussed below) were omitted. The AICPA Special Committee on Accounting Standards Overload (1983) recommended differential measurement and differential disclosure as a means of alleviating the problem of accounting standards overload for small/private businesses. Those statements were accompanied by either an audit, review, or compilation report.

The departures from current GAAP that were contained in the modified GAAP financial statements were:


1.  Accounting for Leases (*FASB Statement 13*)

2.  Capitalization of Interest Cost (*FASB Statement 34*)

3.  Accounting for Compensated Absences (*FASB Statement 43*)

4.  Accounting for Income Taxes (*APB Opinion 11*)[4]

These standards were selected from accounting standards that have been criticized in the literature as not being relevant or cost effective (AICPA 1983, FASB 1983, and Abdel-khalik 1983). Accounting research has also found that these standards are either less useful to bankers in making loan decisions or are not cost effective (Stanga and Tiller 1983, Campbell 1984, Hiltebeitel 1985, and Williams 1987).

The participants were asked to state the line of credit they would grant the subject company and the interest rate they would charge. Once the participants made their decisions concerning the line of credit and interest rate, they were asked to evaluate the risk inherent in the decision, the usefulness of the financial statements in their loan decision, and the additional information that would be required to make the decision using a Likert-scale response. Multivariate analysis of variance was used to test the primary research question and the secondary research questions.

# NOTES

1. The FASB has granted exceptions to some reporting requirements for private and small public companies. The major exceptions are (1) non-public companies are no longer required to report segment information and earnings per share (FASB 1978a), and (2) they are no longer required to disclose pro-forma results for the previous two years when one corporation purchases another (FASB 1984).

2. The committees were the *Committee on Generally Accepted Accounting Principles for Smaller and/or Closely Held Businesses* (1976), the *Special Committee on Small And Medium Sized Firms* (1980), and the *Special Committee on Accounting Standards Overload* (1983).

3. See for example, Stanga and Tiller (1983), Nair and Rittenberg (1983), Knutson and Wichmann (1984), Benson (1985), or Williams (1987).

4. *APB Opinion 11* was superseded by *Statement of Financial Accounting Standards No. 96* (FASB 1987b) which was superseded by *Statement of Financial Accounting Standards No. 107* (FASB 1992). Originally *Statement 96* was to be effective for years ending after December 15, 1988. The implementation of *Statement 96* was delayed three times and in 1992 it was superseded by *Statement No. 107*. *Statement No. 107* is effective for years ending after December 15, 1992 (FASB 1992). *Statements 96* and *107* require that deferred taxes be reported for the difference in the tax basis and the financial statement basis of assets and liabilities. Neither statement provides relief from the problem of accounting standards overload for small businesses.

# II
# LITERATURE REVIEW

Usefulness of information is considered to be the most desirable quality of financial statements. Both the Financial Accounting Standards Board (FASB 1978b) and its predecessor body, the Accounting Principles Board (APB 1970), identified usefulness as the primary ingredient of financial information. The following emphasizes the importance placed on usefulness by these two bodies:

> The basic purpose of financial accounting and financial statements is to provide quantitative financial information about a business enterprise that is useful to statement users, particularly owners and creditors, in making economic decisions. (APB 1970, par. 73)

> Financial reporting should provide information that is useful to present and potential investors and creditors and other users in making rational investment, credit, and similar decisions. (FASB 1978b, par. 34)

The literature and the research concerning accounting for small businesses has addressed the question of whether financial statements prepared in conformance with GAAP are useful to the users of small businesses financial statements. This chapter reviews that literature. The work can be divided into three sections, (1) work performed by the American Institute of Certified Public Accountants, (2) work performed by or for the Financial Accounting Standards Board, and (3) work performed by various individuals or groups. The first section of this chapter reviews the work of the AICPA, the second section reviews the work of the FASB, and the third section reviews the work of individuals and groups.

# STUDIES OF THE AMERICAN INSTITUTE OF CERTIFIED PUBLIC ACCOUNTANTS

Since 1976, the American Institute of Certified Public Accountants has had three separate committees address the problem of accounting standards overload as it relates to small businesses. Although these committees did not perform any "scientific" research, they increased the awareness of the problems that small businesses face when preparing financial statements in conformance with GAAP.

The procedures varied from committee to committee; however, the basic procedures of these committees were: (1) Evidence was gathered by soliciting comments from CPAs and other interested parties concerning the problem of accounting for small businesses. The comments were obtained by either holding discussion forums or by issuing discussion memorandums and soliciting written comments on the discussion memorandums. (2) The evidence was evaluated by the committees through due deliberation and discussion. (3) A final report discussing the committees' findings, conclusions, and recommendations was issued. A discussion of the committees' reports follows.

## *COMMITTEE ON GENERALLY ACCEPTED ACCOUNTING PRINCIPLES FOR SMALLER AND/OR CLOSELY HELD BUSINESSES*

The Committee on Generally Accepted Accounting Principles for Smaller and/or Closely Held Businesses (AICPA 1976) identified owners, owner-managers, and bankers as the primary users of small businesses' financial statements. The Committee concluded that information contained in general-purpose financial statements often is not useful to these groups, but that financial information not ordinarily contained in general-purpose financial statements may have relevance to their decisions. However, the cost of preparing general-purpose financial statements often effectively eliminates the possibility of preparing other more relevant information. The major recommendation of the Committee was:

The Financial Accounting Standards Board should develop criteria to distinguish disclosures that should be required by GAAP, which is applicable to the financial statements of all entities, from disclosures that merely provide additional or analytical data. (Some of these latter disclosures may, however, still be required in certain circumstances for certain types of entities.) The criteria should then be used in a formal review of disclosures presently considered to be required by GAAP and should also be considered by the Board in any new pronouncements. (AICPA 1976, 8-9)

The Committee did not believe that there should be two sets of GAAP, one for smaller and/or closely held businesses and another for large public companies, or that different measurement principles be applied to different businesses based on their size or ownership. However, the Committee did endorse the idea of differential disclosure. Under differential disclosure, large businesses may be required to report additional or analytical data that is not required to be reported by small businesses. For example, the Committee recommended that the FASB amend *APB Opinion No. 15* to require only publicly held companies disclose earnings per share. The Committee believed that disclosure of earnings per share was clearly not relevant to most privately held companies (AICPA 1976, 9). As a result, the Financial Accounting Standards Board issued *Statement of Financial Accounting Standards No. 21* which eliminated the requirement that nonpublic companies report earnings per share and segment information (FASB 1978a).

## THE SPECIAL COMMITTEE ON SMALL AND MEDIUM SIZED FIRMS

The Special Committee on Small and Medium Sized Firms (AICPA 1980) was appointed to address the practice problems of small and medium sized accounting firms. As part of the study of the problems facing small and medium sized accounting firms, the Committee also addressed the problem of accounting standards as they relate to small businesses.

The Committee endorsed the concept of differential disclosure, but rejected the concept of differential measurement. "The Committee concluded that the measurement principles used by entities reporting under GAAP should be the same regardless of the size or character of the company." (AICPA 1980, 13) The Committee also suggested that accounting and auditing standards setting bodies consider the impact of any proposed new standards on small businesses before the standards are adopted.

A final recommendation by the Committee concerning the problem of accounting for small businesses was:

> that the AICPA appoint a special committee to follow up on the work of the AICPA Committee on Generally Accepted Accounting Principles for Smaller and/or Closely held Businesses and to study alternative means of providing further relief for small closely held business from accounting standards which are not cost effective for these businesses. (AICPA 1980, 13)

As a result of this recommendation the AICPA appointed the Special Committee on Accounting Standards Overload.

## SPECIAL COMMITTEE ON ACCOUNTING STANDARDS OVERLOAD

The Special Committee on Accounting Standards Overload (AICPA 1983) considered several different possible solutions to the problem of accounting standards overload as it relates to small businesses. The solutions considered and the reasons the committee did or did not recommend that particular solution were:

1. No change, retain the status quo--The committee rejected this as a possible solution because "the evidence indicates that silent disregard of standards and the abandonment of GAAP are clear and present dangers." (AICPA 1983, 8)

2. Two sets of GAAP--The committee rejected this as a possible solution because "The evidence indicates that there is insufficient support for that solution among users, preparers, or practitioners." (AICPA 1983, 8-9)

3. Optional alternatives to GAAP--The committee evaluated three comprehensive bases of accounting other than GAAP for use by small privately owned businesses. The three bases evaluated were the cash or modified cash basis, the income tax basis, or a new basic accounting method. The committee rejected this as a possible solution because they "cannot provide a broad, long-term solution to the accounting standards overload problem." (AICPA 1983, 14)

4. Simplifying GAAP for all entities--The committee embraced this approach as a solution to the problem of accounting standards. The committee believed that "accounting standards should be simplified and made easier for all entities to apply." (AICPA 1983, 10)

5. Differential disclosure and measurement alternatives-- This is the approach recommended by the committee. The committee did not see this approach as consisting of two sets of GAAP, but as one set of GAAP with added flexibility.

Under an approach based on differential disclosure and differential measurement, the FASB would consider the effects of all standards on small privately held businesses. If the standard would not be relevant for small businesses or would not be cost effective, they could be exempted from its requirements.

When differential disclosure is in use, all businesses measure economic events in the same manner, but additional or analytical information is supplied based on the needs of the users. This approach was recommended by both of the previous AICPA committees that studied the problem of accounting for small businesses. When differential measurement is in use, the manner in which economic events are measured depends on characteristics of the business, such as size or ownership. The Special Committee on Accounting Standards

Overload was the first of the AICPA committees to recommend a solution to the problem of accounting standards overload based on the possibility of differential measurement.

# STUDIES BY THE FINANCIAL ACCOUNTING STANDARDS BOARD

As a result of the 1976 and 1980 committee reports of the American Institute of Certified Public Accountants, the Financial Accounting Standards Board began its own effort to gather information concerning the needs of the users of small and private companies' financial statements. The FASB's effort consisted of two approaches. One approach was the issuance of an invitation to comment entitled *Financial Reporting by Private and Small Public Companies* (FASB, 1981). The responses were published in 1983 (FASB, 1983). The second approach was the sponsoring of a major research study in conjunction with the National Association of Accountants (Abdel-khalik et al. 1983). The principal researcher was A. Rashad Abdel-khalik. These two studies are discussed below.

## *REPORTING BY PRIVATELY OWNED COMPANIES: SUMMARY OF RESPONSES TO FASB INVITATION TO COMMENT*

The FASB issued its invitation to comment, *Financial Reporting by Private and Small Public Companies*, in November 1981 (FASB 1981). The invitation to comment was directed toward three groups, and separate questionnaires were provided for each of these three groups. The three groups were:

1. Managers (including owner-managers) of private and small public companies

2. Users of financial statements of private and small public companies

3. Public accountants providing services to private and small public companies

The invitation to comment was sent to over 15,000 members of the above three groups within the small business community. Responses were received from 283 managers, 193 users (including 154 bankers), and 343 public accountants (FASB 1983, 7-8). The responses were analyzed in an effort to answer seven questions. Following is a discussion of the major findings of the research.

Lenders were identified as the principle external users of small businesses' financial statements. Of the managers responding, 90% responded that their company's financial statements are submitted to external lenders. However, two-thirds of the managers responded that managers are the most important users of their companies' financial statements (FASB 1983, 10).

Bankers indicated that audited financial statements prepared in conformance with GAAP will be required more often for an unsecured loan than for a secured loan (percentages were not given). The bankers also indicated that they would prefer financial statements as their primary source of financial information because:

> information obtained as part of financial statements is believed to be presented better and to have greater reliability in most situations because of a public accountant's association with the financial statements. (FASB 1983, 11-12)

This implies that bankers confuse financial statements that are audited or reviewed with financial statements prepared in conformance with GAAP.

Seventy-one percent (71%) of the lenders reported that they have essentially the same information needs for private as for public companies, and only 22% reported that they rely less on the financial statements of private companies than of public companies. However, 43% of the bankers believe that small companies can account for their activities differently than large companies without reducing the usefulness of their financial statements.

Over 80% of the users indicated satisfaction with small companies' financial statements that are reviewed or audited by public accountants. However, for small companies' financial statements that were compiled, only 50% were "moderately satisfied" (FASB 1983, 17). This suggests that the concern of users of small business financial statements is with the level of accountants' association with the statements and not the accounting principles used in preparation of the statements. The major concern of bankers was that they cannot rely on financial statements that have been compiled by public accountants because they often contain incomplete disclosures (FASB 1983, 27).

In response to the question of whether GAAP should permit different disclosures by private companies than by public companies, 57% of the responding accountants answered "yes." However, 65% of the responding bankers answered "no" (FASB 1983, 26).

The major conclusion of the study is that accountants' perceptions of bank lenders' needs for financial information from small or private companies are fundamentally different from the needs indicated by the users (FASB 1983, 28). However, the needs indicated by the users may not be the same as their actual needs. Bankers frequently (percentages not given) accept GAAP basis financial statements with substantially all disclosures omitted, or accept statements prepared on another comprehensive basis of accounting (FASB 1983, 27).

## FINANCIAL REPORTING BY PRIVATE COMPANIES: ANALYSIS AND DIAGNOSIS

The second method used by the Financial Accounting Standards Board to collect information concerning the problem of accounting by small/private companies was to sponsor a major research study (Abdel-khalik et al., 1983). The research was performed by seven university professors with A. Rashad Abdel-khalik as the principal researcher. The study was partially sponsored by the National Association of Accountants.

Participants in the study were managers, bankers, and accountants. Two groups of managers participated in the study. One group was a random sample of managers of private companies selected from the *Dun & Bradstreet Million Dollar Directory*. The other group consisted of members of the National Association of Accountants who volunteered to participate in the study. A multi-step approach to the research was used. Exploratory interviews with managers, bankers, and accountants were used to identify the essential issues. The exploratory interviews were followed by extensive individual interviews with managers, bankers, and accountants in eight states. The interviews were followed by survey questionnaires. The questionnaires were tailored for the three different groups, although they all addressed the same issues. Follow up interviews with selected bankers and accountants were conducted to clarify the responses to the questionnaire. A discussion of the major findings and conclusions of the research follows.

Both managers in the random survey (68%) and accountants (43%) identified company management as the most important users of small business financial statements. However, bankers were identified as the most important external users of small business financial statements. Other important external users identified were suppliers, bonding agencies, and absentee owners (Abdel-khalik et al. 1983, 45-46).

One of the major questions the study attempted to answer was, "How satisfactory is the information required by GAAP when applied to private companies?" (Abdel-khalik et al. 1983, 7) To answer this question, the perceived effects of using GAAP financial statements were examined. The participants were asked to indicate their agreement or disagreement with several statements concerning the data quality of GAAP basis financial statements and economic consequences of using GAAP basis financial statements.

The bankers agreed that GAAP financial statements provide more understandable data (95% agreed), and are more reliable for use by loan officers (97% agreed). Bankers also agreed, although not as strongly, that the use of GAAP by private businesses would result in less restrictive covenants (57% agreed) and make it easier to finance through debt (65% agreed). However, they did not agree that the use of GAAP financial statements would result in lower borrowing cost (53% disagreed) (Abdel-khalik et al. 1983, 50-51).

Accountants also agreed that the use of GAAP basis financial statements would provide more understandable data (64% agreed), and are more reliable for use by loan officers (69% agreed). However, accountants did not agree that the use of GAAP basis financial statements by private businesses would result in lower borrowing cost (77% disagreed), or less restrictive covenants (68% disagreed). The accountants were evenly split on whether the use of GAAP basis financial statements would make it easier to finance through debt (Abdel-khalik et al. 1983, 50-51).

Bankers indicated that the use of GAAP basis financial statements will result in more reliable and understandable data, and will result in loans with less restrictive covenants with less borrowing cost. However, they "revealed more tolerance of departures from GAAP than would have been deduced from their almost exclusive preference for GAAP." (Abdel-khalik et al. 1983, 2)   When statements are received that are not in conformance with GAAP, bankers can request additional information or take other actions against the borrower such as more restrictive covenants or increased interest rates. However, for four selected GAAP requirements, the bankers reported not taking any action against the borrower when financial statements were not in conformance with GAAP and when requested additional information was not received. The four GAAP requirements and the percentage of time no action was taken are: (1) Capital leases--43%, (2) Interest on construction--45%, (3) Deferred income taxes--28%, and (4) Statement of changes in financial position--41% (Abdel-khalik 1983, 77).

The study also examined the degree of satisfaction with ten current GAAP requirements. The managers and accountants were asked to evaluate the standards based on their complexity and their relevance to decision making. Two of the standards, accounting for deferred income taxes and discounting long-term receivables and payables, were perceived as being both overly complex and not relevant to decisions. Two of the standards, capitalization of interest on construction and accounting for compensated absences, were perceived as less relevant to decisions but not overly complex. Two of the standards, capitalization of leases and accounting for pensions, were seen as overly complex and of somewhat less relevance (Abdel-khalik et al. 1983, 9 & 55-57).

Bankers also "tend to associate GAAP financial statements of private companies with outside accountants." (Abdel-khalik et al. 1983, 2)   Bankers tend to confuse the role of GAAP with the role of outside verification by CPAs in providing useful financial information.


A notable misconception of bankers (which the interviewers frequently had to explain) is the equating of GAAP financial statements with audited financial statements. (Abdel-khalik et al. 1983, 28)

The researchers concluded that private company financial statements are used primarily by managers and bankers and that accountants often assist in the preparation of the statements. Managers use financial statements as aids in decision making and to facilitate borrowing. Bankers use financial statements to provide reliable and understandable data that are helpful in making loan decisions.

They also concluded that departures from GAAP occur with some frequency for certain GAAP requirements especially for small companies. The cost of complying with some GAAP requirements and the perceived lack of relevance to decision making are the reasons for those departures. The problem of accounting for small/private businesses has both a practice problem for accountants and a standard setting problem. A solution to the problem will require the efforts of both the AICPA and the FASB (Abdel-khalik et al. 1983, 1-2).

# STUDIES BY INDIVIDUALS OR GROUPS

In addition to the work performed by the AICPA and the FASB, much work has been performed by individuals and groups. The research has addressed the question of the usefulness of financial statements prepared in conformance with GAAP for small businesses. This section reviews this research.

## *KNUTSON AND WICHMANN*

Knutson and Wichmann (1984) tested whether Certified Public Accountants perceive a difference in the importance of twenty-two disclosure requirements based on the size (small, medium, or large) and the type of company (publicly or privately held). A mail survey was used to conduct the research. Six hundred fifty-nine (659) questionnaires were mailed to practicing accountants in Kentucky and Ohio, and 236 (35%) responded.

The participants were asked to evaluate the importance of twenty-two accounting requirements for four hypothetical manufacturing companies of different sizes and types using a five-point Likert scale ranging from unimportant to essential. The four hypothetical companies were small-private (annual sales of $500,000), medium-private (annual sales of $10,000,000), medium-public (annual sales of $10,000,000), and large-public (annual sales of $500,000,000). An overall hypothesis of no difference for all companies was tested, and individual hypotheses were tested for all possible pairs of companies. Non-parametric statistical tests were used to analyze the data.

The overall hypothesis and three of the four two-way comparisons were rejected for all twenty-two accounting requirements ($p < .05$). The hypothesis that compared the medium-sized-public and the large-public companies was rejected for only one of the twenty-two accounting requirements ($p < .05$).

The authors concluded "that CPAs reject the assumption that most disclosure requirements are equally important for all sizes and types of companies." (Knutson and Wichmann 1984, 46) They also concluded that the findings indicate the accounting requirements are less important for privately owned than for publicly owned companies, are less important for small privately owned than for large privately owned companies, and are of equal importance for medium and large publicly owned companies.

## STANGA AND TILLER

Stanga and Tiller (1983) compared the informational needs of loan officers who make lending decisions for large public companies with the informational needs of loan officers who make lending decisions for small private companies. Stratified sampling was used to divide the participants into a "large bank" group and a "small bank" group. The participants in the "large bank" group were the chief commercial loan officers from the 200 largest banks in the United States. The participants in the "small bank" group were the chief loan officers from the United States banks that ranked in size from 1,001 through 1,200. The participants were divided in this manner because the participants from the "large bank" group should be familiar with the decision process involved in making loans to large companies, and the participants from the "small bank" group should be familiar with the decision process involved in making loans to small companies.

The participants from both groups were asked to evaluate the importance of forty information items using a five-point scale ranging from not important to very important. Both groups received the same questionnaire; however, the "large bank" participants were asked to respond as if they were evaluating a term loan to a large public industrial company and the "small bank" participants were asked to respond as if they were evaluating a term loan to a small private industrial company. The forty information items included twenty-five that are required by GAAP and fifteen that are not required by GAAP.

The hypothesis of no difference in responses between the two groups was tested using the Mann-Whitney U test. The hypothesis was rejected for only ten of the forty items ($p < .05$).

The authors concluded that the study suggests that the information needs of bankers are similar (although not identical) when evaluating loans for small-private or large-public companies. However, several items that are not required to be reported by GAAP were considered more important by both groups than items that are required to be reported. For example, both groups of bankers indicated that forecast of revenue, net income, and capital spending and planned financing are more important than some GAAP requirements including capital lease information and deferred tax information.

## NAIR AND RITTENBERG

Nair and Rittenberg (1983) surveyed accountants, businessmen, and bankers to determine the needs of the users of small businesses' financial statements, and to determine the level of noncompliance with current standards by small businesses. All the participants were from Wisconsin. Descriptive statistics were used to analyze the results.

All three groups of participants were asked to respond to assertions concerning the needs of the users of small businesses financial statements. A five-point scale ranging from substantial disagreement to substantial agreement was used. Results were reported by combining the substantial disagreement and disagreement responses and the substantial agreement and agreement responses into two categories of agreement and disagreement.

The perceptions of the accountants and the businessmen in the survey were similar, and the perceptions of the bankers were different. The bankers were evenly split (46.3% agree; 46.3% disagree) on whether users of small businesses' financial statements rely on financial statements less than do the users of large businesses' financial statements. However, the accountants (46.3% agree; 44.5% disagree) and the businessmen (54.4% agree; 33.8% disagree) felt that users of small businesses' financial statements rely less on financial statements than do the users of large businesses' financial statements.

For the other four assertions concerning users' needs, the responses of the bankers were different from the responses of the accountants and businessmen. For example, the bankers (59.4% disagreed; 18.8% disagreed) disagreed with the assertion, "Users of financial reports of small businesses are more interested in cash flow projections than in the other financial statement information." (Nair and Rittenberg 1983, 88), but the accountants (66.7% agreed) and the businessmen (65.7% agreed) agreed with that assertion.

The bankers were also asked to what extent the financial statements they receive fail to comply with GAAP. Moderate to significant noncompliance with GAAP was reported for 70.9% of the statements without CPA involvement. Noncompliance was reported for 41.8% of compiled statements, 19.3% of reviewed statements, and only 3.4% of audited statements.

The authors concluded that bankers perceive no difference in their needs for financial statement information based on the size of the business. However, CPAs and businessmen do perceive a difference in bankers' needs for financial statement information based on the size of the business.


## CAMPBELL

Campbell (1984) used protocol analysis to evaluate bank loan officers' needs for four items of financial information that was required by GAAP for some companies. The four items of information evaluated were (1) deferred taxes, (2) capital leases, (3) earnings per share, and (4) inflation-adjusted information.

Participants were commercial loan officers from two midwestern banks. Two cases were constructed from the same underlying data. The "Big GAAP" case included the four items of information being evaluated. The "Little GAAP" case did not include any of the four items of information. The participants were asked to evaluate and approve or disapprove a short term, unsecured, $100,000 line of credit. One loan officer at each bank received the "Big GAAP" case, and the other received the "Little GAAP" case. The participants who received the "Little GAAP" case could receive the omitted information upon request. Analysis by components was used to determine what information was processed, and analysis by process was used to determine how the information was processed.

Analysis of the protocols suggests that capitalized lease information was the only one of the four information items evaluated that was useful to the bankers in making the loan decision. Both the "Big GAAP" participants read the capital lease information but only one of the participants verbalized its use. One of the "Little GAAP" participants required the capital lease information before he would make the loan decision.

One of the "Big GAAP" participants mentioned the earnings per share data, but there was no evidence that he used the information as a decision input. None of the other participants mentioned the earnings per share data. One of the "Big GAAP" participants mentioned the deferred tax data, but the evidence suggested that it was not useful in evaluating the requested loan. The other participants did not mention deferred taxes, and the data was not requested by the "Little GAAP" participants.

Neither of the "Little GAAP" participants requested, or mentioned, inflation adjusted information. Both the "Big GAAP" participants evaluated the inflation information, but neither knew how it should be used.

Campbell concluded that inflation information, earnings per share information, and deferred tax information was not useful to the participants in evaluating the requested line of credit. However, the participants were not familiar with the inflation adjusted information and conclusions could not be drawn from this study. The capitalized lease information was useful in this decision context.


## BENSON

Benson (1985) used a two-step research approach to determine what accounting information bankers perceive as useful and to compare their perceptions to what is actually used. The participants were 109 loan officers from small banks in Iowa, Nebraska, and South Dakota. The Federal Reserve Board's definition of "small bank" was used to identify banks considered small.

The first phase of the research was a mail survey. One objective of the survey was to identify GAAP basis accounting information that bankers perceive as useful in the small private company loan decision process. To meet this objective, the participants were asked to evaluate twenty-nine items of accounting information required by GAAP. Responses were obtained using a five-point scale ranging from very useful to not at all useful. The second objective of the survey was to assess the attitudes of bankers concerning the use of GAAP basis accounting by small private companies. To meet this objective, bankers were asked eight questions concerning accounting information that required a "yes" or "no" answer and one question that required a percentage response.

The second phase of the research consisted of participants analyzing a case to make a loan decision. Participants in this stage were eight bankers who responded to the questionnaire in phase one. Protocol analysis was used to analyze the participants processing of the accounting information in evaluating the proposed loan. The purpose of this analysis was to determine if the GAAP basis information items that bankers perceive as useful are actually used in the decision process.

Of the twenty-nine items evaluated in phase one, seven items were perceived as being of high usefulness, sixteen were perceived as being of intermediate usefulness, and six were perceived as being of low usefulness. Three of the six low usefulness items concerned pension plans. The other low usefulness items were information on the company's pollution control expenditures, information concerning changes in the purchasing power of the dollar, and information concerning the accrued liability for future employee absences.

In the second part of the survey, participants reported 59.1% of the financial statements they receive for small businesses are not in conformance with GAAP. The cash basis (34.4%) was the basis used most often. The "yes" or "no" responses to the other questions in this part of the survey were designed to assess bankers' attitudes concerning the use of GAAP by small private companies. The responses to those questions indicate:

1.  That bankers "do not have the same information needs for small private companies as they do for large public companies." (Benson 1985, 209),

2. That "GAAP basis financial statements are received when another basis would have been accepted." (Benson 1985, 208)

3. That "accounting information of small private companies is less useful in making loan decisions than the accounting information of large public companies." (Benson 1985, 212)

4. That bankers "believe that GAAP should be revised to permit small private companies to use different measurement methods." (Benson 1985, 215)

5. That bankers "believe that GAAP should be revised to permit small private companies to have different accounting information disclosures in their financial statements than do large public companies." (Benson 1985, 219)

The second phase of the research used verbal protocols to analyze eight bank loan officers' use of financial information from a hypothetical set of financial statements in context of a loan decision. The purpose of this phase was to confirm or disconfirm the responses to the survey. Three items that were rated as useful in the survey phase of the research were not actually used by the participants in the experimental phase. The three items were information on major purchase commitments, capitalized interest on the balance sheet and income statement, and the rate of growth of earnings per share.

Benson concluded that bankers perceive some GAAP basis accounting information to lack usefulness in the small company loan decision process. These perceptions are supported by the results of the experiment with the exception of the three areas discussed above.

## *HILTEBEITEL*

Hiltebeitel (1985) used an experiment to examine whether the use of different accounting methods by small businesses to measure the same economic events influence the decisions made by bankers. The effects of demographic characteristics on the bankers decisions were also examined. A mail survey was used to conduct the experiment with bankers as subjects.

Each participant received financial statements that were prepared (1) in accordance with GAAP, (2) prepared in conformance with GAAP but the statement of changes in financial position was not presented, (3) included departures from GAAP for accounting for income taxes, accounting for leases, accounting for capitalization of interest, and presentation of the statement of changes in financial position, or (4) included the departures in (3) but the statement of changes in financial position was provided. This resulted in a four-group design. The dependent variables were the participants' risk assessment, the amount of loan approved, the interest rate charged, and their need for additional information. Analysis of variance and linear regression were used to analyze the data.

Results of the statistical tests did not allow rejection of the hypotheses of no difference in the subjects' risk assessment or no difference in their need for additional information between the four groups. However, the hypothesis of no difference in perceived usefulness of the financial statements was rejected. Paired comparisons indicated that the financial statements that omitted all four GAAP requirements were perceived as less useful than the other statements.

Hiltebeitel also examined the effects of several demographic characteristics on the participants assessment of risk. The variables examined were bank size, age, sex, education, experience, employment, and risk aversion. The hypothesis of no difference in risk assessment for the seven variables was rejected for the bank size variable. Bankers from larger banks considered the hypothetical company used in the experiment to be of greater risk than did bankers from smaller banks.

Hiltebeitel concluded that the study supports providing relief to small businesses by allowing them to switch from measurement standards to less complex disclosure standards. He suggests allowing small businesses to disclose information concerning income taxes, leases, and interest cost in the notes to the financial statements instead of in the financial statements themselves.

## WILLIAMS

Williams (1987) examined the relevance and cost effectiveness of four accounting standards. A quasi-experiment was used. Bankers, controllers, and auditors from local, regional, and national firms were the participants. The four accounting standards examined were (1) accounting for leases, (2) capitalization of interest on construction, (3) accounting for deferred taxes, and (4) accounting for compensated absences. Each of the accounting standards was manipulated at two levels, the GAAP alternative and a non-GAAP alternative that has been suggested as more useful for small businesses. This resulted in sixteen independent cases. Each participant evaluated each case for relevance to decision making and cost effectiveness.

The results indicate that the GAAP alternatives are perceived as more relevant than the non-GAAP alternatives. However, they are not perceived as more cost effective. The bankers in the study tend to view the GAAP alternatives as less relevant and less cost effective than do the participants in the other groups. Auditors from national firms tend to view the GAAP alternatives as the most relevant and cost effective. The relationship between the accounting standards was also examined. The GAAP alternative for accounting for leases was perceived as more relevant than the GAAP alternatives for the other three areas. No difference in perceived cost effectiveness was found.

Williams concluded that his study provides some support for allowing small businesses to account for their operations differently than large companies. *Statement of Financial Accounting Concepts No. 2* requires both relevance and cost effectiveness as necessary qualitative characteristics of useful financial information. The study found that none of the four standards examined were perceived as cost effective and only two of the four standards were perceived as relevant. Since *Statement of Financial Accounting Concepts No. 2* requires both relevance and cost effectiveness, there is some support for not requiring the use of the GAAP alternative by small businesses.

## BAKER

Baker (1987) examined the interaction between the accountants' report and basis of accounting. The objective of the study was to examine the effects of different accountants' reports and different bases of accounting on bankers' decisions, and to examine the interaction between accountants' report and basis of accounting. The accountants' report was manipulated at two levels, audit and review. The basis of accounting was also manipulated at two levels, GAAP basis and tax basis. This resulted in a four- group design. Perceptions of bankers concerning the usefulness of statements prepared using the different accounting bases and with different levels of CPA involvement were also examined. A lab experiment with 233 participating bankers was used.

The participants perceived financial statements prepared on the GAAP basis to be more useful than financial statements prepared on the income tax basis. They also perceived the risk of default to be greater if the statements are prepared on the income tax basis. The level of accountants' association with the financial statements also affected the subjects' perceptions. The perceived likelihood of default and the interest rate charged are both higher for reviewed statements than for audited statements. A significant interaction effect was also found. The subjects level of confidence in decisions made using the financial statements was affected by the interaction between the basis of accounting and the accountants' report. Subjects were most confident with audited GAAP basis statements and least confident with audited tax basis statements. Baker interprets this finding as further indication that bankers confuse and mingle the terms "audit" and "GAAP".

## SUMMARY

The work of the committees of the American Institute of Certified Public Accountants served to increase the awareness of the problem of accounting for small businesses. The committees also outlined the issues that needed to be addressed before a solution to the problem could be formulated. The work of the committees also led to the Financial Accounting Standards Board undertaking research to more clearly define the issues and determine if a problem actually existed.

The research of the Financial Accounting Standards Board and much of the earlier work of individuals were opinion surveys. Bankers, practicing CPAs, and managers of small businesses were the participants in these studies. In general, these studies found that when asked, bankers express a desire for financial statements prepared in conformance with GAAP for their small business customers. However, they often accept financial statements prepared on a basis other than GAAP. CPAs on the other hand generally believe that a basis of accounting other than GAAP would be preferable for small businesses.

The differences in what bankers indicate they need and what they are willing to accept from their small business clients led to empirical research designed to determine what information is actually used when bankers evaluate a potential loan for a small business. In general, these studies have found that bankers do not use some of the information contained in GAAP basis financial statements.

One possible explanation of the difference in the results found in the opinion surveys and the results found in the empirical research is that bankers confuse the basis of accounting on which the statements are prepared with the level of outside CPAs' association with the statements. If this is true, a response that GAAP basis financial statements are required could mean that financial statements with a high level of CPA involvement are what are actually required.

This study examined the interaction between the basis of accounting and the level of the external accountants' involvement with the financial statements. The only previous research that examined this relationship was Baker (1987). Baker used tax basis financial statements and GAAP basis financial statements and two levels of accountants' involvement (audit and review). The use of the tax basis of accounting has not been supported by previous research. The AICPA Committee on Accounting Standards Overload (1981) in their tentative conclusions recommended adoption of the tax basis as an alternative to GAAP for small companies. However, the Committee withdrew their support in their final report (AICPA 1983).

This research differed from Baker's research in that the non-GAAP alternative examined was based on the concept of differential measurement and differential disclosure, and three levels of accountants' involvement with the financial statements was examined. Differential measurement and differential disclosure was the approach to solving the accounting standards overload issue recommended by the AICPA Committee on Accounting Standards Overload in their final report (AICPA 1983). This approach was also endorsed by bankers in the Benson study (Benson, 1985).

# III
# RESEARCH METHODOLOGY

The purpose of this chapter is to discuss the methodology used to examine the effects of the type of accountants' report and the basis of accounting on bank loan officers' decisions. The topics discussed in this chapter are: the research questions, the research hypotheses, the participants and the experimental tasks, the independent variables, the dependent variables, the research instrument, and the statistical tests.

## FORMULATION OF THE RESEARCH
## QUESTIONS AND HYPOTHESES

The primary research question addressed in this study was:

1. Does the type of accountants' report and the basis of accounting interact to affect a line of credit decision (i.e., the loan size and interest rate charged) made by bank loan officers when evaluating a loan for a small private company?

As discussed in the first chapter, the primary research question was derived from the conflicting results of prior research, which found that bankers often confuse the basis of accounting on which financial statements are prepared with the level of outside CPA association. Several studies have examined the basis of accounting (Campbell 1984, Benson 1985, Hiltebeitel 1985, and Williams 1987), and two studies (Miller 1985 and Johnson, Pany, and White 1983) have examined the accountants' report. Only one previous study (Baker 1987) examined the interaction of the basis of accounting and the accountants' report.

Baker examined the interaction of the tax basis of accounting and two levels of the accountants' report. This study differs from Baker's by using a modified GAAP basis of accounting instead of the tax basis, and three levels of the accountants' report. The use of a tax basis of accounting has not been supported in previous research and has not been recommended by any committees of the AICPA as an alternative to current GAAP for small/private businesses.

If the type of accountants' report and the basis of accounting do not interact to affect a line of credit decision, then it is important to determine if either affect the decision independently. Therefore, the following questions were investigated:

2. Does the type of accountants' report affect a line of credit decision (i. e. the loan size and interest rate charged) made by bank loan officers when evaluating a loan for a small private company?

3. Does the basis of accounting affect a line of credit decision (i.e., the loan size and interest rate charged) made by bank loan officers when evaluating a loan for a small private company?

Hypotheses one through three are derived from research questions one through three and posit that there will be no difference in loan decisions based on either the accountants' report, the basis of accounting, or the interaction of the two. The hypotheses are:

$H_1$: The type of accountants' report and the basis of accounting have no effect on a line of credit decision (i.e., loan size and interest rate charged) for a small private company.

$H_2$: The type of accountants' report has no effect on a line of credit decision (i.e., loan size and interest rate charged) for a small private company.

H₃: The basis of accounting has no effect on a line of credit decision (i.e., loan size and interest rate charged) for a small private company.

"Reliability concerns the extent to which measurements are repeatable" (Nunnally 1978, 191). The participants in the experiment were asked additional questions and the responses to those questions were used to assess the reliability of the decisions.

Risk is the uncertainty inherent in an investment. As risk increases, the interest rate charged should increase (Weston and Brigham 1974, 283). For a banker, the investment is the loan. If the interest rates recommended are different the perception of risk should be different. Questions four through six examine the participants perceptions of the risk inherent in their decisions and were used to assess the reliability of the participants decisions. Question four examines the interaction of the accountants' report and the basis of accounting on the perceived risk of the decision and questions five and six examine the individual effect of the two variables.

4. Does the type of accountants' report and the basis of accounting interact to affect bank loan officers' perception of risk inherent in a small private company's financial statements?

5. Does the type of accountants' report affect bank loan officers' perception of risk inherent in a small private company's financial statements?

6. Does the basis of accounting affect bank loan officers' perception of risk inherent in a small private company's financial statements?

Hypotheses four through six are derived from research questions four through six. If the responses to the decision variables are reliable, the results of testing hypotheses four through six will be the same as the results obtained from testing hypotheses one through three.

$H_4$:   The type of accountants' report and the basis of accounting have no effect on the perception of risk inherent in a small private company's financial statements.

$H_5$:   The type of accountants' report has no effect on the perception of risk inherent in a small private company's financial statements.

$H_6$:   The basis of accounting has no effect on the perception of risk inherent in a small private company's financial statements.

The primary objective of financial statements is to provide information that is useful in making economic decisions (APB 1970, par. 73 and FASB 1978b, par. 34). A primary quality of useful information is that it have the ability to make a difference in a decision (FASB 1978b). If the different levels of financial statements and accountants' report provide varying levels of information to the participants, the usefulness of the statements will be different for the different groups, and the decisions made using the statements will be different. Questions seven through nine examine the participants perceptions of the usefulness of the financial statements and were used as further assessment of the reliability of the participants decisions.

7.  Does the type of accountants' report and the basis of accounting interact to affect bank loan officers' perceived usefulness of a small private company's financial statements?

8.  Does the type of accountants' report affect bank loan officers' perceived usefulness of a small private company's financial statements?

9.  Does the basis of accounting affect bank loan officers' perceived usefulness of a small private company's financial statements?

Hypotheses seven through nine are derived from research questions seven through nine. If the responses are reliable, the results of testing hypotheses seven through nine will be the same as the results obtained from testing hypotheses one through three.

$H_7$: The type of accountants' report and the basis of accounting have no effect on the perceived usefulness of a small private company's financial statements.

$H_8$: The type of accountants' report has no effect on the perceived usefulness of a small private company's financial statements.

$H_9$: The basis of accounting has no effect on the perceived usefulness of a small private company's financial statements.

Questions ten through twelve were also used as reliability checks and to determine if there was a need for the GAAP basis information not included in the modified GAAP financial statements. If the GAAP basis information is important to the users of the financial statements those who receive the modified GAAP statements should request the GAAP basis information that is not included as well as any information requested by the participants who receive the financial statements prepared in conformance with GAAP.

10. Does the type of accountants' report and the basis of accounting interact to affect bank loan officers' needs for additional information when making a line of credit decision for a small private company?

11. Does the type of accountants' report affect bank loan officers' needs for additional information when making a line of credit decision for a small private company?

12. Does the basis of accounting affect bank loan officers' needs for additional information when making a line of credit decision for a small private company?

Hypotheses ten through twelve are derived from research questions ten through twelve. If the responses are reliable, the results of testing hypotheses ten through twelve will be the same as the results obtained from testing hypotheses one through three.

$H_{10}$:    The type of accountants' report and the basis of accounting have no effect on bank loan officers' needs for additional information when evaluating a loan for a small private company.

$H_{11}$:    The type of accountants' report has no effect on bank loan officers' needs for additional information when evaluating a loan for a small private company.

$H_{12}$:    The basis of accounting has no effect on bank loan officers' needs for additional information when evaluating a loan for a small private company.

## PARTICIPANTS AND EXPERIMENTAL TASKS

Prior research (AICPA 1976, 10; Abdel-khalik et al. 1983, 1; and FASB 1983, 3) identified bank loan officers as the primary external users of small businesses financial statements; therefore, they were used as the participants in this study. According to Casey (1980, 37) bankers:

1.  rely on accounting data in decision making;

2.  analyze financial statements with considerably more sophistication than other large user groups; and

3.  play an influential role in economic resource allocation.

A laboratory study and a mail survey were used to answer the research questions. Randomization was used to assign the subjects to the experimental groups. According to Cook and Campbell (1979, 51-59) the threats to internal validity that randomization does not rule out are imitation of treatments, compensatory equalization, compensatory rivalry, and resentful demoralization of participants receiving less desirable treatments. Since no experimental group received a more desirable treatment (one treatment was not "better" than the other) than another group and there was no competition among the participants, none of these potential threats were present in this study. The major threat to internal validity that may have been present in this study but was mitigated by the use of randomization was the threat due to differences between the kinds of people in one group as opposed to another.

The participants answered a series of thirteen questions based on their evaluation of the financial statements of a small privately held corporation. Two questions required the participants to make a decision based on their analysis of the financial statements. The other questions elicited the perceptions of the participants concerning the financial statements. In addition, the participants answered a series of demographic questions. The independent variables manipulated, the dependent variables, and construction of the research instrument are discussed in following sections.

## INDEPENDENT VARIABLES

Two independent variables were examined in the study, the type of accountants' report and the basis of accounting. The type of accountants' report was included at three levels and the basis of accounting at two levels resulting in a 3 X 2 factorial design. The exhibit on page 13 portrays the research design.

The three types of accountants' report used were an audit report, a review report, and a compilation report. The two bases of accounting used were financial statements prepared in conformance with GAAP and financial statements prepared in conformity with GAAP but modified for four departures from current GAAP requirements.

The departures from current GAAP requirements contained in the modified GAAP statements and the justification for their inclusion in the study are discussed in Chapter 1 on pages 13-14. The modifications were made in a manner often considered more appropriate or more cost effective for small or privately held businesses. The modifications are discussed when the research instrument is discussed in a later section of this Chapter.

Three groups of participants received financial statements prepared in conformance with GAAP including notes to the financial statements (appendix F). The statements were accompanied by either an audit report, review report, or compilation report (appendixes C, D, and E). Three groups of participants received financial statements prepared on a modified GAAP basis including notes to the financial statements (appendix G). Those statements were also accompanied by either an audit report, review report, or compilation report (appendixes C, D, and E). All of the financial statements were for the same company and were based on the same underlying information. All of the participants received the same instructions to participants (appendix A), company description (appendix B), and questionnaire (appendix H).

The level of accountants' association with the financial statements was included as an independent variable because prior research (Abdel-khalik et al. 1983 and FASB 1983) suggests that bankers indicate a preference for financial statements prepared in conformance with GAAP when their actual preference is for financial statements that involve a higher level of outside accountants' association. The three levels of accountants' association with the financial statements are the three levels permissible under the AICPA's professional standards, an audit, a review, and a compilation.

## DEPENDENT VARIABLES

There were two groups of response variables. One group required the participants to make a decision based on the financial statements and the accountants' report that were provided (appendix H, questions 1 and 2). The second group elicited the perceptions of the participants concerning the risk inherent in the financial statements, the usefulness of the financial statements, and the additional information required to make the decision (appendix H, questions 4 through 7).

The decision variables were the line of credit the participant would recommend granting to the subject company and the interest rate to charge (premium above the bank's prime). These are the types of decisions that bankers normally make, and a major input into the decision is the company's financial statements (Casey 1980, 37).

The perception variables were the risk inherent in the loan decision, the perceived usefulness of the different financial statements, and the additional information that would be required to enable the participant to make a decision. The perception variables were included to check the reliability of the responses to the decision variables. The participants responded to their perceptions of these variables using a seven-point Likert scale. The major advantage of a Likert scale is the variance obtained. The major disadvantage is possible biased responses (Isaac and Michael 1981, 142). One possible bias, which is a potential problem in the current study is the central tendency error where the participants rate toward the middle of the scale. An examination of the responses to the perception variables indicate that the central tendency error was not present in the current study.

## THE RESEARCH INSTRUMENT

The financial statements and company description were based on the financial statements of an actual company. The GAAP basis financial statements were prepared in conformance with GAAP (appendix F) in all areas. The modified GAAP basis financial statements (appendix G) were prepared in conformance with GAAP in all areas except the four discussed above. The statements were modified in a manner that has been suggested as more appropriate for small businesses. A discussion of the modifications follows.

Leases that would be considered capital leases under *FASB Statement 13* were handled in conformance with *Statement 13* in the GAAP basis financial statements. In the modified GAAP basis financial statements lease payments were expensed when incurred and no assets or liabilities were established on the balance sheet. The existence of the leases and future minimum lease payments were disclosed in the notes to financial statements.

Interest on construction of the company's asphalt plants was capitalized in conformance with *FASB Statement 34* in the GAAP basis financial statements. In the modified GAAP basis statements all interest was expensed when incurred. An asphalt plant was constructed during the last year covered by the statements. Interest on construction was 10.5% of the total interest for that year and 3.5% of net income. Capitalizing the interest on construction of the plant caused the times interest earned ratio to increase from 4.9 to 5.4. There was disclosure in the summary of significant accounting policies that interest was not capitalized.

In the GAAP basis financial statements a liability was accrued for future compensated absences attributed to services already rendered in conformance with *FASB Statement 43*. In the modified GAAP basis financial statements no liability was accrued, and it was disclosed in the summary of significant accounting policies that no liability for future compensated absences was accrued.

Accounting for income taxes was handled in conformance with *APB Opinion 11* in the GAAP basis financial statements. *APB Opinion 11* was followed instead of *FASB Statement 96* for the following reasons:

1. The original financial statements were prepared in conformance with *APB Opinion 11*.

2. When the experiment was performed *APB Opinion 11* was still in effect. Although *FASB Statement 96* had been adopted but the original effective date was for years beginning after December 15, 1988 (AICPA 1989a, 1).

3. The accounting for deferred taxes question as it relates to small business is not how they should account for deferred taxes, but whether they should account for deferred taxes.

In the modified GAAP basis financial statements the tax expense was the tax on the income tax returns with no accrual of deferred taxes. Determination of the income tax expense was disclosed in the summary of significant accounting policies accompanying the modified GAAP basis financial statements.

Each set of financial statements was accompanied by either an audit, review, or compilation report (appendixes C, D, and E). The report was the same for both the GAAP basis financial statements and the modified GAAP basis statements. *Statement of Auditing Standards No. 58* prescribed a new form of the auditors standard report for reports issued after December 31, 1988 (AICPA 1988). Because the auditors' report that accompanied the financial statements was dated prior to the implementation date of *Statement on Auditing Standards No. 58*, the prior form of the auditors' standard report was used.

All of the participants received the same instructions (appendix A), company description (appendix B), and questionnaire (appendix H). The questionnaire asked for a loan decision based on the financial statements, for the participants perceptions of the risk inherent in the decision, the usefulness of the financial statements, and the need for additional information, and demographic data.

The research instrument was pretested in two steps. The experiment was first administered to a senior auditing class at Louisiana State University during the 1988 summer semester. Forty students participated in the pretest. The participants were asked to comment on the understandability of the instrument, and the amount of time required to complete the instrument was noted. Based on the pretest, questions were restated and the questionnaire was shortened.

After the instrument was modified, the experiment was then administered to six volunteer loan officers at two commercial banks in Baton Rouge, Louisiana. A detailed discussion of the experiment was conducted with two of the loan officers. Final modifications consisted of the rewording of questions and changing the requested line of credit from unsecured to one secured by current assets and property and equipment.

## STATISTICAL TESTS

The discussion of the statistical tests is divided into two parts, test of the decision variables and test of the perception variables. Analysis of the decision variables requires the use of one statistical test, and the analysis of the perception variables requires the use of three statistical tests.

### TEST OF DECISION VARIABLES

To analyze the effects of the independent variables on the decisions of the participants (hypotheses $H_1$, $H_2$, and $H_3$) a 3 X 2 factorial design illustrated in figure 1 was used. Since there are two dependent variables (interest rate and loan amount), two-way multivariate analysis of variance (MANOVA) was used. The general model for the two-way MANOVA is as follows (Johnson and Wichern 1982, 269):

$$\underline{X}_{ijk} = \underline{\mu} + \underline{\Gamma}_i + \underline{B}_j + \underline{\tau}_{ij} + \underline{e}_{ijk}$$

Where:

$\underline{X}_{ijk}$ = the loan granting decision of participant k (a vector of credit line and interest rate), responding to basis of accounting i and accountants' report j.

$\underline{\mu}$ = the overall mean vector for the loan granting decision.

$\underline{\Gamma}_i$ = e effect of the basis of accounting i on the credit line and interest rate.

$\underline{B}_j$ = the effect of the accountants' report j on the credit line and interest rate.

$\underline{\tau}_{ij}$ = the interaction between basis of accounting i and accountants' report j.

$\underline{e}_{ijk}$ = the residual error effect of participant k responding to basis of accounting i and accountants' report k.

$i = 1, 2$

$j = 1, 2, 3$

$k = 1, 2, \ldots,$ number of participants

In multivariate analysis of variance, each treatment has an effect on more than one dependent variable, and the effect of the treatment on all dependent variables is observed simultaneously. If the effects of the treatment are analyzed separately, correlation among the variables is not considered. In MANOVA the simultaneous response to all the variables to the treatment is considered as a single response (Winer

1971, 232). In this experiment each treatment affects both the interest rate and loan amount. MANOVA will consider the response of both variables to the different bases of accounting and accountants' report simultaneously.

## TEST OF PERCEPTION VARIABLES

Hypotheses $H_4$, $H_5$, and $H_6$ were tested using two-way ANOVA since the effects of both the basis of accounting and the accountants' report on the participants' perceptions of risk were considered. The general model for the two-way ANOVA is (Neter, Wasserman, and Kutner 1985, 685):

$$Y_{ijk} = \mu + \Gamma_i + \beta_j + \tau_{ij} + e_{ijk}$$

Where:

$Y_{ijk}$ = the perception of participant k responding to basis of accounting i and accountants' report j.

$\mu$ = the overall mean of the perceptions.

$\Gamma_i$ = the effect of the basis of accounting i.

$\beta_j$ = the effect of the accountants' report j.

$\tau_{ij}$ = the interaction between basis of accounting i and accountants' report j.

$e_{ijk}$ = the residual error effect of participant k responding to basis of accounting i and accountants' report k.

$i = 1, 2$

$j = 1, 2, 3$

$k = 1, 2, \ldots,$ number of participants

The remaining hypotheses were tested using two-way MANOVA. For hypotheses $H_7$, $H_8$, and $H_9$ there were three dependent variables, perceptions of the usefulness of the balance sheet, the income statement, and the statement of cash flows. The general model for the two-way MANOVA is as follows (Johnson and Wichern 1982, 269):

$$\underline{X}_{ijk} = \underline{\mu} + \underline{\Gamma}_i + \underline{B}_j + \underline{\tau}_{ij} + \underline{e}_{ijk}$$

Where:

$\underline{X}_{ijk}$ = the perception participant k of the usefulness of the financial statements (a vector of balance sheet usefulness, income statement usefulness and cash flow statement usefulness), responding to basis of accounting i and accountants' report j.

$\underline{\mu}$ = the overall mean vector for the usefulness perception.

$\underline{\Gamma}_i$ = the effect of the basis of accounting on the perception of usefulness.

$\underline{B}_j$ = the effect of the accountants' report j on the perception of usefulness.

$\underline{\tau}_{ij}$ = the interaction between basis of accounting i and accountants' report j.

$\underline{e}_{ijk}$ = the residual error effect of participant k responding to basis of accounting i and accountants' report k.

$i = 1, 2$

$j = 1, 2, 3$

$k = 1, 2, \ldots,$ number of participants

For hypotheses $H_{10}$, $H_{11}$, and $H_{12}$ there were seven dependent variables. The general model for the two-way MANOVA is as follows (Johnson and Wichern 1982, 269):

$$\underline{X}_{ijk} = \underline{\mu} + \underline{\Gamma}_i + \underline{\beta}_j + \underline{\tau}_{ij} + \underline{e}_{ijk}$$

Where:

$\underline{X}_{ijk}$ = the need of participant k for additional information k (a vector of the seven response variables), responding to basis of accounting i and accountants' report j.

$\underline{\mu}$ = the overall mean vector of the need for additional information.

$\underline{\Gamma}_i$ = the effect of the basis of accounting on the need for additional information.

$\underline{\beta}_j$ = the effect of the accountants' report j on the need for additional information.

$\underline{\tau}_{ij}$ = the interaction between basis of accounting i and accountants' report j.

$\underline{e}_{ijk}$ = the residual error effect of participant k responding to basis of accounting i and accountants' report k.

i = 1, 2

j = 1, 2, 3

k = 1, 2, . . ., number of participants

## SUMMARY

This chapter discussed the methodological procedures used to examine the research questions. The research questions and hypotheses, participants and experimental tasks, independent variables, dependent variables, research instrument, and statistical tests were discussed. The remaining chapters of this dissertation discuss the data analysis, the conclusions to be drawn from the research, and the suggestions for further research.

# IV
# DATA ANALYSIS

The chapter presents the data collection and the results of the statistical analysis described in the previous chapter. The topics discussed in this chapter are: the data collection, analysis of the decision variables, analysis of the perception variables, and demographic data of the participants.

## DATA COLLECTION

The participants in this study were bank loan officers. The participants came from three groups (1) students at the American Bankers Association (ABA) National Commercial Lending School (NCLS), (2) students of the Graduate School of Banking of the South (GSBS), and (3) volunteers from two Florida banks.

### AMERICAN BANKERS ASSOCIATION STUDENTS

The ABA's National Commercial Lending School was held October 22-31, 1988 at Norman, Oklahoma. During registration the students at the school were given a letter explaining the experiment and asking for their voluntary participation (appendix I). The program coordinator for the school also encouraged the students to participate. All of the participants completed the experiment outside class on a voluntary basis, and most of the participants completed the experiment at the time of registration. The different forms of the experiment were distributed to the participants on a random basis. One hundred seventy-nine students were registered in the school, and 114 participated in the experiment providing 103 usable responses.

## GRADUATE SCHOOL OF BANKING STUDENTS

The GSBS supplied a list of ninety-six students of the school and the research instruments were sent to the students on a random basis. The questionnaires were accompanied by a letter from Dr. William F. Staats, the Chair of Banking at Louisiana State University and an instructor in many of the GSBS schools (appendix J). Nine days after the initial mailing, a reminder post card was mailed (appendix K). All of the responses were received within twenty-eight days of the initial mailing. Thirty-two instruments were returned with 30 usable responses.

To test for nonresponse bias in the GSBS group, late responses were used as proxies for nonresponses, and the late responses were compared to the early responses using the Wilcoxon signed ranks test. The Wilcoxon test was performed for all of the response variables for all six experimental groups. There were no differences in the early responses and the late responses for all of the variables ($p > .05$ ).

## VOLUNTEERS

The remaining 14 participants were volunteers from two Florida banks. The subjects were contacted through either the controller or the executive vice-president of the bank. Research instruments were mailed to the officers and were returned by the officers. All instruments mailed were returned.

## SUMMARY OF DATA COLLECTION

The Kruskal-Wallis test was performed to determine if there were any differences in the responses for the three participant groups. The test was performed for all the response variables for the six experimental groups. The results for the decision variables indicate no differences in the responses for all of the decision variables for five of the experimental groups (p-value $> .05$). For the experimental group that received the audited modified GAAP basis statements the hypothesis of no difference in responses was rejected at the .05 level of significance for the interest rate variable.

The results for the perception variables indicate no differences in the responses for all of the perception variables except three (p-value > .05). For the remaining three perception variables the hypothesis of no difference in responses between the three participant groups was rejected at the .05 level of significance. The hypothesis of no difference in responses was rejected for the need for budget information (appendix H, question 7a) for the experimental group that received the audited GAAP basis statements. The hypothesis of no difference was rejected for usefulness of the cash flow statement (appendix H, question 6) for the experimental group that received the compiled GAAP basis statements. The hypothesis of no difference in risk assessment (appendix H, question 3) was rejected for the experimental group that received the audited modified GAAP statements.

Sixty-six tests were performed to test for differences in responses between the three participant groups. Only four (6.1%) of the tests indicated a difference in the responses. Table 1 summarizes the participants in the study.

TABLE 1
SUMMARY OF EXPERIMENTAL PARTICIPANTS

|  | ABA NCLS | GSBS | Other | Total |
|---|---|---|---|---|
| Potential participants | 179 | 96 | 14 | 289 |
| Actual participants | 114 | 32 | 14 | 160 |
| Useable responses | 103 | 30 | 14 | 147 |
| Useable response rate - percent | 57.5 | 31.2 | 100.0 | 50.9 |

# ANALYSIS OF THE DECISION VARIABLES

The main purpose of this study was to determine whether the type of accountants' report and the basis of accounting interact to affect a line of credit decision made by bank loan officers when evaluating a loan for a small private company. To examine this question, the participants in the study were given a set of financial statements prepared either in accordance with GAAP or in accordance with a modified GAAP basis of accounting. Each set of financial statements was accompanied by either an audit report, review report, or compilation report. (See appendixes C, D, E, F, and G.) The participants were asked to indicate the maximum line of credit they would recommend for the company and the interest rate they would charge. This is a 3 X 2 factorial design. The mean responses by cell for both the amount of the line of credit and interest rate charged are shown in table 2. The 3 X 2 factorial design with two response variables requires the use of multi-variate analysis of variance (MANOVA).

TABLE 2
SUMMARY OF RESPONSES TO DECISION VARIABLES

|  |  |  | Basis of Accounting | |
|---|---|---|---|---|
|  |  |  | GAAP | Modified GAAP |
| Type of Report | Audit | Amount | $230,083 | $198,750 |
|  |  | Rate | 1.885% | 1.917% |
|  | Review | Amount | $232,708 | $202,083 |
|  |  | Rate | 1.833% | 1.927% |
|  | Compilation | Amount | $212,917 | $193,542 |
|  |  | Rate | 1.896% | 1.917% |

## TESTS OF THE ASSUMPTIONS OF MANOVA

The assumptions underlying the use of MANOVA are:

1. The components of the error term vectors should have a bivariate normal distribution, and

2. The covariance matrices are equal for all groups (Johnson and Wichern 1982).

Bivariate normality of the error term vectors was examined first since the test for equal covariance matrices (Bartlett's test) is sensitive to nonnormality (Johnson and Wichern 1982, 245). Before bivariate normality can be examined, univariate normality must be examined. If the data are not univariate normal, it will not be bivariate normal (Johnson and Wichern 1982, 151-156). The univariate normality of the data within each cell and the univariate normality of all the combined data were examined.

The Statistical Analysis System (SAS) was used for the data analysis in this study. SAS uses the Shapiro-Wilk's test statistic to test for univariate normality when the number of observations is fifty or less and the Kolmogorov-Smirnov D-statistic when the number of observations is greater than fifty. Therefore, the Shapiro-Wilk's test was used to test the univariate normality of the data within the six experimental cells, and the Kolmogorov-Smirnov test was used to test for univariate normality of the combined data.

The test of the univariate normality of the data within each cell resulted in rejection of the null hypothesis of normally distributed error terms for nine of the twelve variables (six cells with two variables per cell) at the .01 level of significance. The test of the univariate normality of the combined data resulted in rejection of the hypothesis of normally distributed error terms for both variables at the .01 level of significance.

Bartlett's test for equal covariance matrices is sensitive to nonnormality (Johnson and Wichern 1982, 245). In practice, nonnormality and unequal covariance matrices tend to occur at the same time, but the transformation that corrects the problems of nonnormality often helps correct the problem of unequal covariance matrices (Neter, Wasserman, and Kutner 1985, 616).

Using the Box-Cox methodology (Box and Cox, 1964), an exponential transformation to near normality was attempted. The Box-Cox methodology is used to find the best possible exponential or logarithm transformation that would transform the data to near normality. The Box-Cox procedure indicated that the best possible transformation would be an exponential transformation using -.4 as the exponent for both the amount and rate variables. Therefore, both the amount and rate variables were transformed using -.4 as the exponent.

Although the Box-Cox procedure finds the best possible transformation, its use does not assure that the data will be transformed to near normality. Therefore, the transformed data must be tested for normality. As was done for the original data, the transformed data was tested for normality within each cell and for the combined data. The Shapiro-Wilk's test indicated that the null hypothesis of normally distributed error terms within each cell was rejected for eight of the twelve variables (six cells with two variables per cell) at the .01 level of significance. The Kolmogorov-Smirnov test indicated that the null hypothesis of normally distributed error terms was rejected for both the combined variables at the .01 level of significance. Since no transformation to near normality was found, Bartlett's test for equality of variance covariance matrices was not attempted.

There is no nonparametric equivalent to MANOVA and no transformation to near normality could be found. When data violate the assumptions of the usual parametric test and there is no nonparametric equivalent:

> The recommended procedure ... is to use the usual analysis of variance on the data and then to use the same procedure on the rank transformed data. If the two procedures give nearly identical results the assumptions underlying the usual analysis of variance are likely to be reasonable and the regular parametric analysis valid. When the two procedures give substantially different results, the analysis on ranks is probably more accurate than the analysis on the data and should be preferred. (Conover 1980, 337)

Therefore, MANOVA was performed on both the data and on the rank transformed data. The result of ranking is a procedure that is conditionally distribution free. However, the procedure results in a level of significance that is fairly close to the approximate level of significance no matter what the underlying population distribution may be (Conover 1980, 337). The following section reports the results of MANOVA performed on both the original data and on the rank transformed data.

## *RESULTS OF THE STATISTICAL TESTS*

The total sample size of 147 resulted in unequal cell sizes. Three of the cells had twenty-five participants and three of the cells had twenty-four participants. One procedure that is used when cell sizes are unequal is to randomly omit observations in order to reduce all cells to the same size which allows conventional analysis on the data (Kirk 1982, 415). Observations were randomly omitted from the three cells with twenty-five participants before the analysis was performed.

Table 3 reports the results of the MANOVA for both the original data and the ranked data. When SAS is used to perform MANOVA the F-statistic is calculated using four methods (Wilks' Criterion, Pillai's Trace, Hotelling-Lawley Trace, and Roy's Maximum Root Criterion). The four test criteria gave similar results for both the original data and the ranked data for all the tests reported; therefore, only the Pillai's Trace statistic is reported in the exhibits in this chapter.

TABLE 3
OVERALL RESULTS OF MANOVA - DECISION VARIABLES

| Hypothesis | Original Data | | Ranked Data | |
|---|---|---|---|---|
| | F Value | P Value | F Value | P Value |
| Type of report- $H_2$ | .18 | .9462 | .25 | .9089 |
| Basis of accounting-$H_3$ | .88 | .4167 | 1.06 | .3484 |
| Report*Basis- $H_1$ | .15 | .9638 | .32 | .8620 |

There are no significant differences between the MANOVA performed on the ranked data and the MANOVA performed on the original data. The results of both procedures are failure to reject the null hypotheses of no differences in loan decisions attributable to different basis of accounting or type of accountants' report or the interaction of the two ($H_1$, $H_2$, and $H_3$).

## DISCUSSION OF THE RESULTS

The results of this study are generally consistent with the results of prior studies which found that neither the basis of accounting nor the accountants' report affect decisions by bank loan officers. Prior studies have considered either the basis of accounting or the accountants' report, and one study considered the interaction of the two.

### Basis of Accounting

Several studies compared decisions made using financial statements prepared in accordance with GAAP with decisions made using financial statements prepared with departures from GAAP. The results of these studies are consistent with the results of the current study.

Benson (1985) found that bank loan officers perceive information on accrued compensated absences to be of low usefulness. He also found that bankers do not use capitalized interest information when making loan decisions.

Hiltebeitel (1985) found no differences in decisions made by loan officers using financial statements prepared in accordance with GAAP and financial statements prepared with departures from GAAP in three areas. The areas that were modified were accounting for leases, accounting for income taxes, and accounting for capitalized interest.

Campbell (1984) used protocol analysis and found that deferred tax information was not considered by the participants in making loan decisions. However, she did find that capitalized lease information was processed by the participants in making loan decisions. She did not determine if the use of the information made a difference in the participants decisions. Lin (1988) used an interactive computer experiment and found no differences in loan decisions when capitalized lease information was presented and when capitalized lease information was not presented.

The results of the present study are consistent with the results of the prior studies except for Campbell (1984) which found that capitalized lease information was processed by loan officers when making loan decisions. For financial information to be useful it must be both relevant and reliable (FASB 1980). For accounting information to be relevant "it must be capable of making a difference in a decision" (FASB 1980, par 47). Other studies (Hiltebeitel 1985 and Lin 1988) found that the inclusion or exclusion of capital lease information from the financial statements made no differences in bank loan officers' loan decisions. Although capitalized lease information was processed by loan officers in Campbell's study, other studies (including the present study) indicate that the information is not useful for decision making.

*Accountants' Report*

Two studies (Johnson, Pany, and White 1983 and Miller 1985) have considered the effect of the independent accountants' report on decisions of bank loan officers. Johnson, Pany, and White (1983) found that the level of outside CPA involvement did not affect the loan officers' decisions. Miller (1985) did find a difference in loan officers' decisions made when the financial statements were accompanied by a compilation report compared to the decisions made when the financial statements were accompanied by an audit report. The differences were in the amount of the loan and not the interest rate. However, he found no differences in an audit report and a review report and a review report and a compilation report. Although there were no statistically significant differences found in the current study for the three levels of outside CPA association, the amount of the loan allowed was greater for audit and review reports than for compilation reports.

*Interaction of Basis of Accounting and CPA Involvement*

Baker (1987) examined the interaction of basis of accounting and outside CPA involvement. The statements were prepared in conformance with GAAP or on the income tax basis, and they were accompanied by either an audit report or a review report. Baker found that basis of accounting and outside CPA involvement did interact to affect the decision of bank loan officers. However, Baker's subjects were not familiar with audited income tax basis statements; therefore, he concluded that the interaction was caused by that unfamiliarity. In the present study the modified GAAP statements did not look so "unusual" to the participants; therefore, their appearance would not have affected their decisions.

# ANALYSIS OF THE PERCEPTION VARIABLES

This study also investigated whether bank loan officers' perceptions of the financial statements differed based on the different levels of outside CPA association and the different bases of accounting. The three perceptions evaluated were, (1) the perceptions of the risk inherent in the loan decision, (2) the perceptions of the usefulness of the financial statements, and (3) the perceived need for additional information required to make the decision.

A Likert scale was used to measure the perception variables. Therefore, the measurements are from the ordinal measurement scale and do not meet the assumptions of the ratio measurement scale which is required for use of ordinary parametric tests (Pfaffenberger and Patterson 1977, 670). The test of the perception of risk inherent in the loan decision requires the use of a 2 X 3 ANOVA, and the tests of the perceptions of the usefulness of the financial statements and the additional information require the use of 2 X 3 MANOVA. There are no nonparametric equivalents to these two parametric tests. In the manner recommended by Conover (1980, 337) and used earlier to test for differences in the decision variables, the parametric tests were performed on both the original data and the rank transformed data and the results compared. The results are shown in the following sections.

## TEST OF THE RISK INHERENT IN THE LOAN DECISION

Question 3 on the questionnaire (appendix H) asked the participants to assess the risk inherent in their line of credit decision. The responses were used to test hypotheses $H_4$, $H_5$, and $H_6$. ANOVA was performed on both the original data and the ranked data and the results are presented in Table 4 on the following page.

TABLE 4
OVERALL RESULTS OF ANOVA - PERCEPTIONS OF RISK

| Hypothesis | Original Data | | Ranked Data | |
|---|---|---|---|---|
| | F Value | P Value | F Value | P Value |
| Type of report- $H_5$ | .46 | .5003 | .42 | .5196 |
| Basis of accounting-$H_6$ | 1.60 | .2047 | 1.63 | .2000 |
| Report*Basis- $H_4$ | .01 | .9907 | .00 | .9995 |

These results are consistent with the results for the decision variables. As risk increases, the interest rate charged should increase (Weston and Brigham 1974, 283). Therefore, if the different levels of basis of accounting or accountants' association with the financial statements resulted in different assessment of risk this should have resulted in different loan decisions.

In addition to testing for differences in the risk assessment, Spearman's rho was calculated to determine the correlation between the risk assessment and the interest rate charged and the amount of the loan. There was a positive correlation between the risk assessment and both the interest rate charged and the loan amount (for loan amount rho = .24, p = .005 for interest rate charged rho = .17, p = .05). This indicates that as the perceptions of risk increased the amount of the loan decreased and the interest rate charged decreased. It also indicates that the participants took the task seriously and that the responses are reliable.

## TEST OF THE USEFULNESS OF THE FINANCIAL STATEMENTS

Questions 4, 5, and 6 on the questionnaire (appendix H) asked the participants to assess the usefulness of the three financial statements. The responses were used to test hypotheses $H_7$, $H_8$, and $H_9$. MANOVA was performed on both the original data and the ranked data, and the results are shown in table 5.

TABLE 5
OVERALL RESULTS OF MANOVA
PERCEPTIONS OF USEFULNESS

| Hypothesis | Original Data | | Ranked Data | |
|---|---|---|---|---|
|  | F Value | P Value | F Value | P Value |
| Type of report- $H_8$ | .93 | .4770 | 1.11 | .3583 |
| Basis of accounting-$H_9$ | 2.58 | .0564 | 2.03 | .1121 |
| Report*Basis- $H_7$ | .18 | .9822 | .28 | .9444 |

The results are different for the ranked data and the original data for the basis of accounting main effect. The analysis for the original data indicates that the basis of accounting may have affected the perceived usefulness of the financial statements. The analysis of the ranked data indicates that the basis of accounting did not affect the perceived usefulness of the financial statements. According to Conover (1980, 337), "When the two procedures give substantially different results, the analysis on the ranks is probably more accurate than the analysis on the data and should be preferred." However, additional tests were performed to provide additional evidence concerning whether there were differences in the perceived usefulness of the statements.

To determine which of the three financial statements may have caused any differences in the perceived usefulness, ANOVA was performed using the perception of the usefulness of each of the financial statements as the dependent variable on both the original data and the ranked data. The ANOVAs performed for the perceived usefulness of the balance sheet and the income statement indicate no differences for the perceived usefulness of either of the two statements caused by either the type of report, the basis of accounting, or the interaction of the two (p > .10). The ANOVA results for the third statement (cash flow) are shown in table 6.

TABLE 6
ANOVA TEST OF USEFULNESS
OF CASH FLOW STATEMENT

| Hypothesis | Original Data | | Ranked Data | |
|---|---|---|---|---|
| | F Value | P Value | F Value | P Value |
| Type of report | .50 | .6077 | .57 | .5663 |
| Basis of accounting | 3.70 | .0564 | 3.16 | .0777 |
| Report*Basis | .50 | .6077 | .56 | .5714 |

The ANOVA on both the original data and the ranked data indicates a possible difference in the perceived usefulness of the cash flow statement caused by the basis of accounting. Tukey's HSD (Kirk 1982, 116-7) test was used to evaluate all pairwise comparisons to determine if there were any differences between the cells. At the .05 level of significance, there were no differences found between any of the cells.

Although a statistically significant difference in the perceived usefulness of the cash flow statement was not found, the differences caused by the basis of accounting was greater for the cash flow statement than for the balance sheet and the income statement. A possible explanation is that the cash flow statement was prepared in compliance with *FASB Statement No. 95* (FASB 1987a) using the indirect method of presentation. *Statement No. 95* was effective for years ending after July 15, 1988 with earlier application encouraged. *Statement No. 95* had been in effect for only three months when most of the participants completed the experiment. It is possible that they were not familiar with the format of the statement and how it should be used, thus causing the differences in the responses.

These results are consistent with the results for the decision variables. As the usefulness of the financial statements changes, the decisions made using the financial statements should change. The results indicate no differences in the usefulness of the statements and no differences in the decisions made.

In addition to testing for differences in the perceived usefulness of the financial statements, Spearman's rho was calculated to determine the correlation between the loan amount recommended and the perceived usefulness of the financial statements. There was a positive correlation (for the balance sheet rho = .22, p = .01; for the income statement rho = .15, p = .05; for the statement of cash flow rho = .05, p = .58) between the amount of the loan recommended and the perceived usefulness of all three of the financial statements. The correlation between the perceived usefulness of the cash flow statement and the amount of the loan was not statistically different from zero. As discussed above this may have been caused by the participants unfamiliarity with the statement of cash flows prepared in accordance with *Statement 95*

## TEST OF THE ADDITIONAL INFORMATION REQUIRED

Question 7a through 7g on the questionnaire (appendix H) asked the participants what additional information would be required to make a decision on the loan request. The responses were used to test hypotheses $H_{10}$, $H_{11}$, and $H_{12}$. MANOVA was performed on both the original data and the ranked data, and the results are in table 7.

TABLE 7
OVERALL RESULTS OF MANOVA - ADDITIONAL
INFORMATION REQUIRED

|  | Original Data | | Ranked Data | |
| --- | --- | --- | --- | --- |
| Hypothesis | F Value | P Value | F Value | P Value |
| Type of report-$H_{11}$ | .50 | .9321 | .37 | .9820 |
| Basis of accounting-$H_{12}$ | .88 | .5279 | 1.28 | .2646 |
| Report*Basis-$H_{10}$ | .64 | .8303 | .65 | .8172 |

These results are consistent with the results for the decision variables and the other perception variables. The results indicate no differences in the need for additional information between the six experimental groups.

Questions 7f and 7g (appendix H) asked the participants to indicate their need for any additional information concerning specific financial statement items (7f) and their need for any other additional information useful in their decision (7g). Some of the participants included non-financial statement items in 7f; therefore, the responses were analyzed together. Table 8 on the following page lists the six items of additional information requested most frequently. A chi-square test was used to determine whether the frequency of requests differed among the six treatment groups.

These six items are not required to be contained in financial statements prepared in conformance with GAAP. This supports the Committee on Generally Accepted Accounting Principles for Smaller and/or Closely Held Businesses (AICPA 1976) conclusion that information not ordinarily contained in general-purpose financial statements may have more relevance to bankers decisions than some information that is required to be reported by GAAP.

Of the participants that received the modified GAAP basis financial statements, only one indicated a need for detailed information on leases. No need was indicated for additional information in the areas of interest capitalization and compensated absences. Four participants did indicate a need for copies of the corporation's tax returns; however, two of the participants received the GAAP basis statements and two received the modified-GAAP basis statements.

Seven of the participants who received reviewed or compiled statements indicated a need for a higher level of outside CPA involvement. Four of the participants who received GAAP basis financial statements and a review or compilation report indicated a need for audited statements. Three of the participants who received modified GAAP basis financial statements and a compilation report indicated a need for audited or reviewed statements.

TABLE 8
ADDITIONAL INFORMATION REQUESTED

| Information requested | Number | Percent of Total Responses | P-Value for Chi-square Test |
|---|---|---|---|
| Aging of accounts receivable | 62 | 43.1 | * |
| List and appraisal of property and equipment | 26 | 18.1 | .23 |
| Aging of accounts payable | 24 | 16.7 | .21 |
| Schedule of work-in-process | 21 | 14.6 | * |
| Cash budget for coming year | 14 | 9.7 | * |
| Monthly detail of prior year cash flow | 12 | 8.3 | * |

\* -- p-value greater than .25
144 total responses

## DISCUSSION OF THE RESULTS

The results for the perception variables are consistent with the results of the decision variables. The different bases of accounting and the different levels of outside CPA involvement did not affect the decisions made by the participants, nor did they affect the perceptions of the risk involved in the loan, the usefulness of the financial statements, or the need for additional information. With one exception (discussed above) the correlation between the perception variables and the decision variables was positive. This indicates that the participants took the task seriously and that the responses are reliable.

The additional information requested also supports the statistical results of no differences in the experimental groups. The six items of additional information requested most often (table 8) were not items normally contained in GAAP basis financial statements. If the data omitted from the modified GAAP basis financial statements were important in the decision making, it would have been requested by the participants who received the modified GAAP statements. The omitted data were not requested. This is an additional indication that the GAAP basis information did not affect the participants decisions.

# DEMOGRAPHIC DATA OF THE PARTICIPANTS

Questions 8 through 15 of the questionnaire (appendix H) were used to collect demographic data. The participants came from thirty-nine states. The data was analyzed using the demographic data as the independent variable and the decision variables as the dependent variables to determine if any of the demographic data affected the responses. Since the decision variables were not normally distributed and no transformation to near normality was found, the analysis was performed on both the original data and the rank transformed data. Discussion of the demographic data is divided as follows: experience and education, bank size and title, and loan amount.

## *EXPERIENCE AND EDUCATION*

Question 8 asked the participants for their experience as a bank loan officer. Six of the participants did not respond to the question; the remaining participants were experienced loan officers. The average experience of the participants in each group is summarized in table 9 on the following page.

ANOVA was performed using experience as the dependent variable to determine if the participants' experience was different for the different experimental groups. Before performing ANOVA the experience variable was transformed to near normality using an exponential transformation of -.10. The results indicate no difference in experience between the six experimental groups (p > .52).

TABLE 9
EXPERIENCE AS A BANK LOAN OFFICER

| Experimental Group | Average in Years |
|---|---|
| GAAP basis - audit report | 7.05 |
| GAAP basis - review report | 8.86 |
| GAAP basis - compilation report | 6.25 |
| Modified GAAP basis - audit report | 5.35 |
| Modified GAAP basis - review report | 5.85 |
| Modified GAAP basis - compilation report | 8.02 |
| Average for all participants | 6.92 |

Question 13 asked the participants for their education level. The responses are summarized in table 10.

TABLE 10
EDUCATION LEVEL

| Education | Number | Percent |
|---|---|---|
| Some college | 32 | 22.2 |
| Bachelors degree | 63 | 43.8 |
| Some graduate work | 28 | 19.4 |
| Masters degree | 17 | 11.8 |
| No response | 4 | 2.8 |

MANOVA was used to test for the effect of experience and education on the loan decision. The amount of the loan and the interest rate charged were the independent variables. MANOVA was performed on both the original data and the rank transformed data. Before performing MANOVA the experience of the participants was combined into four groups using the 25th, 50th and 75th percentile as the dividing points. The results are shown in table 11.

TABLE 11
OVERALL RESULTS OF MANOVA
EDUCATION AND EXPERIENCE

| | Original Data | | Ranked Data | |
|---|---|---|---|---|
| Hypothesis | F Value | P Value | F Value | P Value |
| Type of report | .20 | .9756 | .25 | .9601 |
| Basis of accounting | 1.01 | .4193 | .84 | .5437 |
| Report*Basis | .56 | .9225 | .72 | .7930 |

The results of the MANOVA indicate that neither education nor experience affected the participants loan granting decision, nor did they interact to affect the decision.

## BANK SIZE

Question 14 of the questionnaire (Appendix H) asked the participants for the total assets of their bank. Table 12 on the following page summarizes the responses.

TABLE 12
BANK SIZE

| Total Assets | Number | Percent |
| --- | --- | --- |
| Under $25 million | 4 | 2.8 |
| $25 to $50 million | 18 | 12.5 |
| $50 to $100 million | 33 | 22.9 |
| $100 to $500 million | 39 | 27.1 |
| $500 million to $1 billion | 17 | 11.8 |
| Over $1 billion | 28 | 19.4 |
| No response | 5 | 3.5 |

A one-way MANOVA was performed on both the original data and the rank transformed data using bank size as the independent variable and the loan decision as the dependent variable. The results indicate that bank size did not affect the loan decision (for the original data p-value = .8965; for the ranked data p-value = .7445).


## TITLE

Question 9 of the questionnaire (appendix H) asked the participants their current job title. Table 13 on the following page summarizes the responses. The other category consisted of seven different job titles including branch manager, investment manager, and manager of commercial lending.

A one-way MANOVA was performed on both the original data and the rank transformed data using job title as the independent variable and the loan decision as the dependent variable. The results indicate that current job title did not affect the loan decision (for the original data p-value = .7511; for the ranked data p-value = .7629).

TABLE 13
JOB TITLE

| Title | Number | Percent |
|-------|--------|---------|
| President | 6 | 4.2 |
| Vice president | 84 | 58.2 |
| Loan officer | 24 | 16.7 |
| Other | 26 | 18.1 |
| No response | 4 | 2.8 |

## NORMAL LOAN SIZE

Question 12 of the questionnaire (appendix H) asked the participants the size of the loan they normally approve. Several of the participants indicated that they had either no authority to approve any loans individually, or that they only had authority to approve small loans individually and that large loans were approved by a committee. The responses were analyzed using the amounts approved by the committee, if both the committee amount and the individual amount were given. The range of responses was $5,000 to $1,700,000.

One-way MANOVA was performed on both the original data and the rank transformed data using the amount of the loan normally approved as the independent variable and the loan decision as the dependent variable. Before performing MANOVA the responses of the participants were combined into four groups using the 25th, 50th and 75th percentile as the dividing points.

The MANOVA results indicate that the amount of the loan normally approved did affect the loan decision (for the original data p-value = .0268; for the ranked data p-value = .0062). Tukey's HSD test (Kirk 1982, 116-7) was used to evaluate all pairwise comparisons to determine if there were any differences between the cells. At the .05 level of significance, no differences were found between any of the cells for interest rate charged. At the .05 level of significance there was a difference found between the group that normally approves large loans and the other three groups. The participants that normally approve the largest loans approved a larger loan than the participants in the other three groups.

## SUMMARY OF THE RESULTS

The participants in this study were not a random sample of the population of bank loan officers. However, they do represent a wide variety of geographic location, level of education, experience level, bank size, and size of loan normally reviewed or approved. The participants could be considered experienced loan officers. (The average experience in reviewing and approving loans was 6.92 years). There was no difference in the experience of the participants between the experimental groups. There were also no material differences in the responses of the participants between the ABA students, the GSBS students, and the volunteers.

The analysis presented in this chapter indicates that the basis of accounting and the level of outside CPA association with the financial statements had no effect on the loan granting decision of the participants. The analysis also indicates that the basis of accounting and the level of outside CPA association had no effect on their perceptions of risk involved in the loan granting decision, the usefulness of the financial statements, or their need for additional information. This indicates that the responses are consistent and reliable.

The analysis of the demographic data indicates that only one of the demographic variables had an effect on the loan decisions of the participants. The participants who are normally involved with the largest loans recommended a higher line of credit than the participants in the other three groups.

# V
# SUMMARY AND CONCLUSIONS

This chapter is an overall summary of the research study and the implications of the results. Limitations of the research and suggestions for further research are also considered.

## SUMMARY AND IMPLICATIONS

Small business is an important sector of the United States economy. However, accounting standards are promulgated with the needs of the financial analysts and stockholders of public companies in mind (AICPA 1976, AICPA 1981), and the accounting needs of companies at the small end of the size spectrum are often overlooked when standards are established (AICPA 1983, 2). These problems have led to concern that small companies are required to provide information that is either not needed or not used by the users of their financial statements and that the cost of providing this information precludes small companies from providing other more useful information (FASB 1981, 1).

The AICPA, the FASB, and private individuals or groups have devoted considerable effort to studying the problems of accounting for small businesses. Two committees of the AICPA (1976, 1983) have recommended that either differential disclosure, differential measurement, or both be adopted by the FASB to help alleviate the accounting problems of small business. However, the FASB has done little to alleviate the problem of accounting for small businesses. Since 1983, the date of the last AICPA committee report, the FASB has issued thirty-eight Statement of Financial Accounting Standards. In general, these standards are applicable to small and privately held businesses as well as large publicly held businesses. During that time period there has been little effort to lessen the burden of accounting standards overload on small or privately held business.

*Statement of Financial Accounting Concepts No. 2* (FASB 1980) indicates that accounting information is only useful if it is both relevant and reliable. To be relevant, accounting information "must be capable of making a difference in a decision" (FASB 1980, par 47). Earlier empirical studies have compared the relevance of financial statements prepared in conformance with GAAP to financial statements prepared with some GAAP requirements omitted or to financial statements prepared on some other comprehensive basis of accounting. These studies have found that the use of financial statements prepared in accordance with GAAP did not result in different decisions than the use of financial statements prepared with departures from GAAP in areas where current requirements are believed to be either unnecessary or costly for small/private businesses (Benson 1985 and Hiltebeitel 1985).

This study expands on the prior research by adding as an independent variable the level of outside CPA association with the financial statements. Early survey research in the area of accounting for small businesses found that bankers were more concerned with the level of outside CPA involvement than the basis of accounting on which small business financial statements were prepared (FASB 1983 and Abdel-khalik et al. 1983). Therefore, the level of outside CPA involvement was added as a variable to determine if there were any differences in the decisions made.

This study found no differences in decisions made using financial statements prepared in conformance with GAAP compared to decisions made using financial statements prepared without the burdensome requirements of four current GAAP requirements. The information required to be reported by current GAAP in the four areas examined did not make a difference in the decisions of the participants in this study; therefore, in this study, it was not relevant. This is consistent with prior studies and is a violation of the FASB's own *Statement of Financial Accounting Concept No. 2* (FASB 1980) which requires that useful information be able to make a difference in a decision. Also, the participants who received the modified GAAP basis financial statements did not request the GAAP basis information which was omitted.

The cost to small business of complying with the current GAAP requirements is greater than the cost of applying the modified GAAP alternative. In this study the GAAP basis information did not make a difference in the participants decisions; therefore, it was not useful. *Statement of Financial Accounting Concept No. 2* requires that the benefits of information should exceed its cost (FASB 1980, par 33). If the information is not useful for decision making, there are no benefits to compare to the cost; therefore, the requirement that benefits exceed cost is violated.

Although generalizing the results of this study to other situations or other GAAP requirements (discussed below) may not be warranted, the results indicate that small businesses should be relieved of the burden of current GAAP requirements in the four areas examined. If information is not used in decision making, there is no reason to incur the cost required to produce that information. Small businesses have limited resources to use in providing accounting and other financial information. If they are relieved of the burden of current GAAP requirements in the four areas studied, the resources currently being devoted to those areas could be devoted to other areas.

In this study the level of outside CPA association with the financial statements did not affect the loan decision. When this study is considered along with the prior research, the results are not clear concerning the effect of CPA involvement on loan decisions. Johnson, Pany, and White (1983) found that the level of outside CPA involvement did not affect the interest rate decision made by bank loan officers. However, Miller (1985) found that there was a difference in the loan amount between an audit report and a compilation report. Miller found no difference in the loan amount between an audit report and a review report and no differences between a review report and a compilation report. Miller found no difference in the interest rate charged. This study is consistent with the prior studies, with the exception of Miller finding a difference in an audit report and a compilation report for the loan amount.

This research has implications for two groups. First, the FASB should reconsider whether to continue to require small/private businesses to account for their operations in the same manner as large publicly held businesses in the four areas which were examined. This study found that the information provided by the GAAP requirements examined did not make a difference in decision making. This is in violation of the FASB's own *Statement of Financial Accounting Concept No. 2*. Since there is a cost involved in complying with the current GAAP requirements in the areas studied, the FASB should consider allowing small businesses to use a modified GAAP method of accounting in these areas. This will lower their accounting cost and allow them to devote their resources to other areas.

The 1983 Special Committee on Accounting Standards Overload of the AICPA (1983) recommended that small businesses be allowed to account for their operations using differential measurement and differential disclosure. The FASB has not adopted the principle of differential measurement but has adopted the principle of differential disclosure in a limited number of areas. The results of this study provide support for the use of both differential measurement and differential disclosure by small/private companies in the four areas studied.

The second group for which the research has implications is the owner/managers of small privately held businesses and the CPAs who serve those businesses. If the current GAAP requirements do not result in a higher loan amount or lower interest rate, they should consider using some other method of accounting if doing so will help to decrease accounting costs.

The implications are also important when owner/managers of small privately held businesses and the CPAs who serve those businesses decide on the level of CPA association with the financial statements. If a higher level of CPA involvement does not affect the amount that a small/private business can borrow or the cost of borrowing, the business should consider having the least costly level of CPA involvement with their financial statements.

## LIMITATIONS OF THE RESEARCH

As with any experiment, the participants were asked to make decisions in an artificial environment. In an actual lending decision the participants would have more information and more time to make the decision. In many cases loan officers are asked to approve a given line of credit or loan instead of recommending a line of credit of any amount, and often the actual decision is made by a loan committee instead of the individual loan officers. Random assignment of the participants to the experimental groups mitigates the threats to the internal validity caused by different loan granting methods used by the participants (Cook and Campbell 1979, 56). Random assignment does not decrease the threats to external validity. In an effort to minimize this problem, the financial statements of an actual company were used and the company description was based on that company. Nevertheless, this may affect generalization of the study.

A second limitation is that the financial statements used were for a construction company. Virtually all sectors of the United States economy include small private businesses. Generalization of the results to business in industries other than construction may not be appropriate.

Only four accounting standards were modified in the modified GAAP basis financial statements. Generalization of the results to other standards that have been criticized as not appropriate for small private businesses is not warranted.

The accountants' reports accompanying the modified GAAP basis financial statements did not contain qualifications because of the departures from GAAP. Current auditing and accounting and review standards would require a qualification. If the qualification had been contained in the reports, the results of the study may have been different.

## SUGGESTIONS FOR FUTURE RESEARCH

The suggestions for future research are derived from the limitations to the current research discussed above. A future study should replicate the current study, but have the decisions made by groups to simulate decisions made by loan committees. This would more closely reflect how loan officers actually make decisions, and would increase the possibility that the manipulated variables were actually processed by at least one of the decision makers.

Use of financial statements of a company operating in a different industry would also be beneficial. It is possible that information not important to bank loan officers when making a loan decision for a construction company is important when making a loan decision for a company in another industry. Performing a similar experiment with financial statements of a company in another industry may help answer this question.

The current study examined only four accounting standards. A future study should examine other accounting standards to determine if the information generated by the current GAAP requirements is used in decision making. The study could also be replicated using another basis of accounting, such as the modified cash basis.

Finally, the study should be replicated with qualifications in the accountants' reports accompanying the modified GAAP basis financial statements. If the results were different, it would indicate that the wording of the accountants' report is important information.

# APPENDIX A
# INSTRUCTIONS TO
# PARTICIPANTS

The purpose of this study is to evaluate the usefulness of certain accounting information to bank loan officers when evaluating a business loan. The results of the study should be useful to bank loan officers as well as accountants. Responses will be confidential. Your responses will be used only for the purposes of the study and in conjunction with responses from other participants. A summary of the results will be available to participants.

The following information for APC Construction Company, Inc. is attached:

1. Description of the company

2. Accountants' report

3. Financial statements

4. Notes to the financial statements

Please review the attached information before answering the questionnaire. The following information should be considered while reviewing the attached information and answering the questions.

1. APC Construction Company, Inc. is seeking a short-term line of credit to be used to meet cash flow requirements during peak operating periods of 1988.

2. The line of credit will be secured by current assets or by property and equipment.

3. APC Construction Company, Inc. is not currently a customer of your bank, but your bank will become their main depository after the line of credit is granted.

4. You are familiar with the CPA firm associated with the Company's financial statements and have a favorable opinion of their work.

5. Your bank has money available to lend.

After reviewing the attached information, turn to the questionnaire and answer the questions. In an actual loan situation you would have more information available. However, please answer the questions to the best of your ability given the information available.

## THANK YOU FOR YOUR PARTICIPATION

# APPENDIX B
# COMPANY DESCRIPTION

APC Construction Company, Inc. is a privately owned corporation engaged in asphalt paving and excavating. Work is performed under fixed price contracts for both governmental and private customers. The normal operating cycle of the business is less than one year. Contracts are obtained early in the calendar year. As soon as weather permits, work on the contracts is started, with most jobs completed by December 1. By January 31 of the following year, virtually all of the receivables have been collected and all trade accounts paid. The company's contract revenues have grown at an average rate of 16% during the last four years. It is anticipated that this growth rate will continue into the near future.

All of the outstanding stock is owned by Ben Hogan and Jeremiah Johnson. Each owns 50% of the stock. Both owners are actively involved in operating the corporation on a daily basis. Neither have substantial outside interests. Hogan is president of the corporation, Johnson is vice-president; however, responsibility is shared equally. Hogan and Johnson started the business eleven years ago as a partnership. The business was incorporated in January 1984. Johnson and Hogan were each paid salaries of $46,000 for both 1987 and 1986. The salaries of the owners are included as part of the general and administrative expenses on the income statement.

Many of the small contracts do not call for progress payments to be made while the work is in progress, so the company must wait until the contract is complete to collect. Virtually all the contracts that do permit progress payments require that 10% of the contract amount be retained by the customer until the contract is complete and the work accepted. Since materials must be purchased, equipment rented, and employees paid throughout the year, this results in negative cash flow during much of the operating cycle. The company has managed the problem in the past by delaying payments to suppliers and key employees, including the owners. Because of the growth of the company, this no longer appears to be a viable solution to the cash flow problem. The company is now seeking a short-term line of credit that can be used during periods that cash disbursements exceed cash receipts. The company anticipates drawing on the line of credit during periods of negative cash flows, then repaying the loan at the end of the operating cycle when most accounts have been collected.

# APPENDIX C
# AUDIT REPORT

Stockholders and Board of Directors
APC Construction Company, Inc.

We have examined the balance sheet of APC Company, Inc. as of December 31, 1987 and 1986, and the related statements of income and retained earnings and cash flows for the years then ended. Our examination was made in accordance with generally accepted auditing standards and, accordingly, included such tests of the accounting records and such other auditing procedures as we considered necessary in the circumstances.

In our opinion the financial statements referred to above present fairly the financial position of APC Company as of December 31, 1987 and 1986 and the results of its operations and its cash flows for the years then ended, in conformity with generally accepted accounting principles applied on a consistent basis.


Vance and Richards
Certified Public Accountants


February 8, 1988

# APPENDIX D
# REVIEW REPORT

Stockholders and Board of Directors
APC Construction Company, Inc.

We have reviewed the accompanying balance sheet of APC Construction Company, Inc. as of December 31, 1987 and 1986 and the related statements of income and retained earnings and cash flows for the year then ended, in accordance with standards established by the American Institute of Certified Public Accountants. All information included in the financial statements is the representation of the management of APC Construction Company, Inc.

A review consists principally of inquiries of company personnel and analytical procedures applied to financial data. It is substantially less in scope than an examination in accordance with generally accepted auditing standards, the objective of which is the expression of an opinion regarding the financial statements taken as a whole. Accordingly, we do not express such an opinion.

Based on our review, we are not aware of any material modifications that should be made in the accompanying financial statements in order for them to be in conformity with generally accepted accounting principles.

Vance and Richards
Certified Public Accountants

February 8, 1988

# APPENDIX E
# COMPILATION REPORT

Stockholders and Board of Directors
APC Construction Company, Inc.

We have compiled the accompanying balance sheet of APC Construction Company, Inc. as of December 31, 1987 and 1986 and the related statements of income and retained earnings and cash flows for the years then ended, in accordance with standards established by the American Institute of Certified Public Accountants.

A compilation is limited to presenting in the form of financial statements information that is the representation of management. We have not audited or reviewed the accompanying financial statements, and accordingly, do not express an opinion or any other form of assurance on them.

Vance and Richards
Certified Public Accountants

February 8, 1988

# APPENDIX F
# GAAP BASIS
# FINANCIAL STATEMENTS

APC CONSTRUCTION COMPANY, INC.
BALANCE SHEET
December 31, 1987 and 1986

*ASSETS*

|  | 1987 | 1986 |
|---|---|---|
| CURRENT ASSETS: |  |  |
| Cash | $ 264,317 | $ 189,612 |
| Accounts receivable: |  |  |
| Currently due, net of $15,580 and |  |  |
| $7,000 allowance for |  |  |
| uncollectible accounts | 119,711 | 24,867 |
| Retainage | 63,976 | 41,681 |
| Cost and estimated earnings in excess of |  |  |
| billings on uncompleted contracts | 29,769 | 24,452 |
| Prepaid expense | 55,374 | 30,132 |
| Total current assets | 533,147 | 310,744 |
| PROPERTY AND EQUIPMENT, net of |  |  |
| accumulated depreciation and amortization | 639,348 | 557,747 |
| Total assets | $1,172,495 | $ 868,491 |

APC CONSTRUCTION COMPANY, INC.
BALANCE SHEET
December 31, 1987 and 1986

*LIABILITIES AND STOCKHOLDERS' EQUITY*

|  | 1987 | 1986 |
|---|---|---|
| **CURRENT LIABILITIES:** | | |
| Accounts payable | $ 187,697 | $ 90,929 |
| Notes payable, current portion | 82,944 | 107,377 |
| Lease obligations, current portion | 19,919 | 17,747 |
| Billings in excess of cost and estimated | | |
|     earnings on uncompleted contracts | 14,809 | 1,283 |
| Accrued expenses | 45,628 | 89,406 |
| Accrued income taxes | 99,750 | 55,100 |
| Total current liabilities | 450,747 | 361,842 |
| **OTHER LIABILITIES:** | | |
| Notes payable, noncurrent | 196,713 | 118,905 |
| Lease obligations, noncurrent | 31,652 | 51,571 |
| Deferred taxes | 31,627 | 16,617 |
| Total other liabilities | 259,992 | 187,093 |
| Total liabilities | 710,739 | 548,935 |
| **STOCKHOLDERS' EQUITY:** | | |
| Common stock, $1 par value, 50,000 shares | | |
| authorized, issued, and outstanding | 50,000 | 50,000 |
| Additional paid-in capital | 105,316 | 105,316 |
| Retained earnings | 306,440 | 164,240 |
| Total stockholders' equity | 461,756 | 319,556 |
| Total liabilities and | | |
| stockholders' equity | $1,172,495 | $ 868,491 |

The accompanying notes are an integral part of these statements.

## APC CONSTRUCTION COMPANY, INC.
## STATEMENT OF INCOME AND RETAINED EARNINGS
### For the Years Ended December 31, 1987 and 1986

|                                                                 | 1987 | 1986 |
|-----------------------------------------------------------------|------|------|
| Contract revenues earned                                        | $3,768,576 | $3,188,984 |
| Cost of revenues earned                                         | 3,170,585 | 2,735,470 |
| Gross profit                                                    | 597,991 | 453,514 |
| General and administrative expenses                             | 315,531 | 277,777 |
| Income from operations                                          | 282,460 | 175,737 |
| Other income (expense):                                         |      |      |
|   Interest and rent income                            | 14,712 | 19,319 |
|   Gain on sale of equipment                           | 7,355 | 4,180 |
|   Interest expense, net of capitalized interest of $4,740 for 1987 | (47,567) | (37,843) |
|   Total other income (expense)                        | (25,500) | (14,344) |
| Income before tax                                               | 256,960 | 161,393 |
| Provision for income taxes                                      | 114,760 | 65,246 |
| Net income                                                      | 142,200 | 96,147 |
| Retained earnings, beginning of year                            | 164,240 | 68,093 |
| Retained earnings, end of year                                  | $ 306,440 | $ 164,240 |

The accompanying notes are an integral part of these statements.

APC CONSTRUCTION COMPANY, INC.
STATEMENT OF CASH FLOWS
For the Years Ended December 31, 1987 and 1986

|  | 1987 | 1986 |
|---|---|---|
| Cash flows from operating activities: | | |
| Net income | $ 142,200 | $ 96,147 |
| Adjustments to reconcile net income to net cash provided by operating activities: | | |
| Depreciation and amortization | 210,220 | 218,364 |
| Gain on sale of equipment | (7,355) | (4,180) |
| Changes in assets and liabilities: | | |
| Change in total accounts receivable | (117,139) | 10,437 |
| Change in cost and earnings in excess of billings | (5,317) | (16,391) |
| Change in prepaid expenses | (25,242) | 1,870 |
| Change in accounts payable | 96,768 | 21,389 |
| Change in billings in excess of cost and earnings | 13,526 | (25,417) |
| Change in accrued expenses | (43,778) | 15,141 |
| Change in accrued income taxes | 44,650 | 11,867 |
| Change in deferred income taxes | 15,010 | 10,146 |
| | | |
| Net cash provided by operating activities | 323,543 | 339,373 |

## APC CONSTRUCTION COMPANY, INC.
## STATEMENT OF CASH FLOWS
### For the Years Ended December 31, 1987 and 1986

|  | 1987 | 1986 |
|---|---|---|
| Cash flows from investing activities: | | |
| Purchase of property and equipment | (298,742) | (232,303) |
| Sale of equipment | 14,276 | 4,180 |
| Net cash used in investing activities | (284,466) | (228,123) |
| Cash flows from financing activities: | | |
| Proceeds from long-term notes | 173,350 | 104,557 |
| Payment of long-term notes | (119,975) | (173,582) |
| Principal payments on capital leases | (17,747) | (15,812) |
| Net cash provided (used) in financing activities | 35,628 | (84,837) |
| Net increase in cash | 74,705 | 26,413 |
| Cash at beginning of year | 189,612 | 163,199 |
| Cash at end of year | $ 264,317 | $ 189,612 |

The accompanying notes are an integral part of these statements.

APC CONSTRUCTION COMPANY, INC.
NOTES TO FINANCIAL STATEMENTS
December 31, 1987 and 1986

*Note 1 - Significant Accounting Policies*

(A) *Income on construction contracts*

The company recognizes revenues on construction contracts for financial reporting purposes and for tax purposes, based on the "percentage-of-completion" method of accounting. Revenue is recognized as work on the contracts progress. Revenues recognized are based on the ratio of costs incurred to the total estimated costs.

(B) *Property and equipment*

Property and equipment are stated at historical cost. Interest cost incurred in connection with construction of the company's asphalt plants is capitalized. For financial reporting purposes, the assets are depreciated using the straight-line method over useful lives of 3 to 12 years. Property under capital lease is amortized over the terms of the leases.

Depreciation and amortization expense of $210,220 for 1987 and $194,020 for 1986 included amortization of $18,798 each year.

(C) *Income taxes*

Deferred income taxes are provided for differences in timing in reporting of expenses for financial statement and tax purposes arising from differences in the methods of accounting for capital leases and depreciation. Investment tax credits are applied as a reduction to the current provision for federal income taxes using the flow-through method.

## Note 2 - Income Taxes and Deferred Income Taxes

For the years ended December 31, 1987 and 1986, the provision for taxes on income consisted of the following:

|  | 1987 | 1986 |
|---|---|---|
| Currently payable, net of investment credit of $8,486, and $6,908 | $ 99,750 | $ 55,100 |
| Deferred |  |  |
| Related to depreciation | 15,557 | 11,698 |
| Related to capital leases | (547) | (1,552) |
| Tax expense | $114,760 | $ 65,246 |

At December 31 of the respective years, the components of the balance of deferred income taxes were:

|  | | |
|---|---|---|
| Related to depreciation | $ 35,134 | $ 19,577 |
| Related to capital leases | (3,507) | (2,960) |
|  | $ 31,627 | $ 16,617 |

## Note 3 - Property and Equipment

|  | 1987 | 1986 |
|---|---|---|
| Assets |  |  |
| Machinery and equipment | $ 985,018 | $ 866,198 |
| Autos and trucks | 403,482 | 378,263 |
| Asphalt plants | 416,445 | 300,618 |
| Furniture and fixtures | 28,426 | 14,010 |
| Property under capital lease | 93,988 | 93,988 |
|  | 1,927,359 | 1,653,077 |
| Less accumulated depreciation and amortization | 1,288,011 | 1,095,330 |
| Net property and equipment | $ 639,348 | $ 557,747 |

## Note 4 - Lease Obligations

The company leases certain construction equipment under leases classified as capital leases. The company's shop and office building is leased from the two stockholders under a lease classified as an operating lease. The following is a schedule showing the future minimum lease payments under capital leases by years and the present value of the minimum lease payments at December 31, 1987:

| Year ending December 31, | |
|---|---|
| 1988 | $25,853 |
| 1989 | 25,853 |
| 1990 | 9,940 |
| Total minimum lease payments, capital leases | 61,646 |
| Less: | |
| Amount representing executory cost | 2,371 |
| Amount representing interest | 7,704 |
| Present value of minimum lease payments | $51,571 |

The operating lease, which expires August 31, 1991, does not include an option to renew. Future minimum lease payments for the operating lease are as follows:

| Year ending December 31, | |
|---|---|
| 1988 | $22,800 |
| 1989 | 22,800 |
| 1990 | 22,800 |
| 1991 | 15,200 |
| Total minimum lease payments, operating leases | $83,600 |

Rental expense resulting from short-term rentals of equipment included in cost of revenues earned were $117,078 for 1987 and $120,708 for 1986. Rental expense of $22,800 resulting from rent of the shop and office was included in general and administrative expenses for both 1987 and 1986.

*Note 5 - Notes Payable*

|  | 1987 | 1986 |
|---|---|---|
| Notes payable to banks and finance companies with varying interest rates, maturities, and repayment schedules | $279,657 | $226,282 |
| Less current maturities | 82,944 | 107,377 |
|  | $196,713 | $118,905 |

*Note 6 - Cost and Estimated Earnings on Uncompleted Contracts*

|  | 1987 | 1986 |
|---|---|---|
| Costs incurred on uncompleted contracts | $473,316 | $297,610 |
| Estimated earnings | 89,655 | 54,212 |
|  | 562,971 | 351,822 |
| Less: Billings to date | 548,011 | 326,807 |
|  | $ 14,960 | $ 25,735 |

|  | | |
|---|---|---|
| Included in the accompanying balance sheet under the following captions: | | |
| Costs and estimated earnings in excess of billings | $ 29,769 | $ 24,452 |
| Billings in excess of costs and estimated earnings | (14,809) | (1,283) |
|  | $ 14,960 | $ 25,735 |

# APPENDIX G
# MODIFIED GAAP BASIS
# FINANCIAL STATEMENTS

APC CONSTRUCTION COMPANY, INC.
BALANCE SHEET
December 31, 1987 and 1986

*ASSETS*

|  | 1987 | 1986 |
|---|---|---|
| **CURRENT ASSETS:** | | |
| Cash | $ 264,317 | $ 189,612 |
| Accounts receivable: | | |
| Currently due, net of $15,580 and $7,000 allowance for | | |
| uncollectible accounts | 119,711 | 24,867 |
| Retainage | 63,976 | 41,681 |
| Cost and estimated earnings in excess of billings on uncompleted contracts | 29,769 | 24,452 |
| Prepaid expense | 55,374 | 30,132 |
| Total current assets | 533,147 | 310,744 |
| **PROPERTY AND EQUIPMENT**, net of accumulated depreciation | 584,539 | 487,581 |
| Total assets | $1,117,686 | $ 798,325 |

## LIABILITIES AND STOCKHOLDERS EQUITY

|                                                              | 1987        | 1986       |
|--------------------------------------------------------------|-------------|------------|
| **CURRENT LIABILITIES:**                                     |             |            |
| Accounts payable                                             | $ 187,697   | $ 90,929   |
| Notes payable, current portion                               | 82,944      | 107,377    |
| Billings in excess of cost and estimated earnings on uncompleted contracts | 14,809      | 1,283      |
| Accrued expenses                                             | 27,406      | 75,729     |
| Accrued income taxes                                         | 99,750      | 55,100     |
| Total current liabilities                                    | 412,606     | 330,418    |
| **OTHER LIABILITIES:**                                       |             |            |
| Notes payable, noncurrent                                    | 196,713     | 118,905    |
| Total liabilities                                            | 609,319     | 449,323    |
| **STOCKHOLDERS' EQUITY:**                                    |             |            |
| Common stock, $1 par value, 50,000 shares authorized, issued, and outstanding | 50,000      | 50,000     |
| Additional paid-in capital                                   | 105,316     | 105,316    |
| Retained earnings                                            | 353,051     | 193,686    |
| Total stockholders' equity                                   | 508,367     | 349,002    |
| Total liabilities and stockholders' equity                   | $1,117,686  | $ 798,325  |

The accompanying notes are an integral part of these statements.

APC CONSTRUCTION COMPANY, INC.
STATEMENT OF INCOME AND RETAINED EARNINGS
For the Years Ended December 31, 1987 and 1986

|  | 1987 | 1986 |
|---|---|---|
| Contract revenues earned | $3,768,576 | $3,188,984 |
| Cost of revenues earned | 3,170,878 | 2,737,212 |
| Gross profit | 597,698 | 451,772 |
| General and administrative expenses | 315,454 | 277,674 |
| Income from operations | 282,244 | 174,098 |
| Other income (expense): | | |
| Interest and rent income | 14,712 | 19,319 |
| Gain on sale of equipment | 7,355 | 4,180 |
| Interest expense | (45,196) | (28,797) |
| Total other income (expense) | (23,129) | (5,298) |
| Income before tax | 259,115 | 168,800 |
| Provision for income taxes | 99,750 | 55,100 |
| Net income | 159,365 | 113,700 |
| Retained earnings, beginning of year | 193,686 | 79,986 |
| Retained earnings, end of year | $ 353,051 | $ 193,686 |

The accompanying notes are an integral part of these statements.

## APC CONSTRUCTION COMPANY, INC.
## STATEMENT OF CASH FLOWS
For the Years Ended December 31, 1987 and 1986

|                                                        | 1987 | 1986 |
|--------------------------------------------------------|---------:|---------:|
| Cash flows from operating activities:                  |          |          |
| Net income                                             | $ 159,365 | $ 113,700 |
| Adjustments to reconcile net income to net cash provided by operating activities: |  |  |
| Depreciation                                           | 190,124  | 198,562  |
| Gain on sale of equipment                              | (7,355)  | (4,180)  |
| Changes in assets and liabilities:                     |          |          |
| Change in total accounts receivable                    | (117,139) | 10,437  |
| Change in cost and earnings in excess of billings      | (5,317)  | (16,391) |
| Change in prepaid expenses                             | (25,242) | 1,870    |
| Change in accounts payable                             | 96,768   | 21,389   |
| Change in billings in excess of cost and earnings      | 13,526   | (25,417) |
| Change in accrued expenses                             | (48,323) | 11,724   |
| Change in accrued income taxes                         | 44,650   | 11,867   |
| Net cash provided by operating activities              | 301,057  | 323,561  |

APC CONSTRUCTION COMPANY, INC.
STATEMENT OF CASH FLOWS
For the Years Ended December 31, 1987 and 1986

|  | 1987 | 1986 |
|---|---|---|
| Cash flows from investing activities: |  |  |
| Purchase of property and equipment | (294,003) | (232,303) |
| Sale of equipment | 14,276 | 4,180 |
| Net cash used in investing activities | (279,727) | (228,123) |
| Cash flows from financing activities: |  |  |
| Proceeds from long-term notes | 173,350 | 104,557 |
| Payment of long-term notes | (119,975) | (173,582) |
| Net cash provided (used) in financing activities | 53,375 | (69,025) |
| Net increase in cash | 74,705 | 26,413 |
| Cash at beginning of year | 189,612 | 163,199 |
| Cash at end of year | $ 264,317 | $ 189,612 |

The accompanying notes are an integral part of these statements.

APC CONSTRUCTION COMPANY, INC.
NOTES TO FINANCIAL STATEMENTS
December 31, 1987 and 1986

*Note 1 - Significant Accounting Policies*

(A) *Income on construction contracts*

The company recognizes revenues on construction contracts for financial reporting purposes and for tax purposes, based on the "percentage-of-completion" method of accounting. Revenue is recognized as work on the contracts progress. Revenues recognized are based on the ratio of costs incurred to the total estimated costs.

(B) *Property and equipment*

Property and equipment are stated at historical cost. Asphalt plants were constructed by the company. No interest cost was capitalized in the years in which the plants were constructed, including the year ended December 31, 1987. For financial reporting purposes the assets are depreciated using the straight-line method over useful lives of 3 to 12 years.

Depreciation expense was $190,120 for 1987 and $174,218 for 1986.

(C) *Income taxes*

Income tax expense is the tax due per the federal and state tax returns. For financial statement purposes, property and equipment are depreciated using the straight-line method. Accelerated methods including the Accelerated Cost Recovery System (ACRS) are used for tax purposes. Deferred income taxes have not been determined for the differences in taxable income and net income per the financial statements. Taxable income per the tax returns was $233,932 for 1987 and $141,436 for 1986.

Investment tax credits are applied as a reduction to the current provision for federal income taxes using the flow-through method.

(D) *Compensated absences*

Employees are entitled to paid vacation based on length of service. No liability has been reported in the balance sheet for compensation for future absences.

*Note 2 - Income Taxes*

|  | 1987 | 1986 |
|---|---|---|
| Taxes computed at the statutory rates | $108,236 | $ 62,008 |
| Less investment credit | 8,486 | 6,908 |
| Tax expense | $ 99,750 | $ 55,100 |

*Note 3 - Property and Equipment*

|  | 1987 | 1986 |
|---|---|---|
| Assets |  |  |
| Machinery and equipment | $ 985,018 | $ 866,198 |
| Autos and trucks | 403,482 | 378,263 |
| Asphalt plants | 401,061 | 289,973 |
| Furniture and fixtures | 28,426 | 14,010 |
|  | 1,817,987 | 1,548,444 |
| Less accumulated depreciation | 1,233,448 | 1,060,863 |
| Net property and equipment | $ 584,539 | $ 487,581 |

*Note 4 - Lease Obligations*

The company leases certain construction equipment under long-term leases. The shop and office building is leased from the two stockholders under a long-term lease. All long-term leases are accounted for as operating leases. The leases for the construction equipment expire March 1990 and August 1990 and do not contain an option to renew. The lease for the shop and office building expires August 31, 1991 and does not contain and option to renew. Following is a schedule showing the future minimum lease payments under long-term leases for construction equipment and for shop and office building at December 31, 1987:

Construction equipment:
Year ending December 31,

| | |
|---|---:|
| 1988 | $ 25,853 |
| 1989 | 25,853 |
| 1990 | 9,940 |
| Total minimum lease payments, construction equipment | $ 61,646 |

Shop and office building:
Year ending December 31,

| | |
|---|---:|
| 1988 | $ 22,800 |
| 1989 | 22,800 |
| 1990 | 22,800 |
| 1991 | 15,200 |
| Total minimum lease payments, building | $ 83,600 |

Total all long-term leases:
Year ending December 31,

| | |
|---|---:|
| 1988 | $ 48,653 |
| 1989 | 48,653 |
| 1990 | 32,740 |
| 1991 | 15,200 |
| Total minimum lease payments, all leases | $145,246 |

Rental expense of $142,931 and $146,561 resulting from rentals of equipment were included in cost of revenues earned for 1987 and 1986 respectively. Rental expense of $22,800 resulting from rent of the shop and office was included in general and administrative expenses for both years.

*Note 5 - Notes Payable*

| | 1987 | 1986 |
|---|---:|---:|
| Notes payable to banks and finance companies with varying interest rates, maturities, and repayment schedules | $279,657 | $226,282 |
| Less current maturities | 82,944 | 107,377 |
| | $196,713 | $118,905 |

*Note 6 - Cost and Estimated Earnings on Uncompleted Contracts*

|  | 1987 | 1986 |
|---|---|---|
| Costs incurred on uncompleted contracts | $473,316 | $297,610 |
| Estimated earnings | 89,655 | 54,212 |
|  | 562,971 | 351,822 |
| Less: Billings to date | 548,011 | 326,807 |
|  | $ 14,960 | $ 25,735 |

Included in the accompanying balance sheet under the following captions:

| Costs and estimated earnings in | | |
|---|---|---|
| excess of billings | $ 29,769 | $ 24,452 |
| Billings in excess of costs | | |
| and estimated earnings | (14,809) | (1,283) |
|  | $ 14,960 | $ 25,735 |

# APPENDIX H
# QUESTIONNAIRE

Please answer the following questions after you have examined the attached financial statements and company description.

1. Based on the attached financial statements, what is the maximum line of credit you would recommend for this company? (This cannot be a range. It must be a single number.)

   _____

2. What interest rate premium (amount above the bank's prime rate) would you recommend for this line of credit? (This cannot be a range. It must be a single number.)

   _____

3. Based on the attached financial statements, how would you rate the riskiness of the recommended line of credit at the recommended interest rate?

   Extremely                                    Extremely
     Safe     1      2      3      4      5      6      7     Risky

4. How useful was the attached balance sheet in making your line of credit and interest rate decisions?

    Extremely                                                          Not
       Useful   1       2       3       4       5       6       7   Useful

5. How useful was the attached income statement in making your line of credit decisions?

    Extremely                                                          Not
       Useful   1       2       3       4       5       6       7   Useful

6. How useful was the attached statement of cash flows in making your line of credit and interest rate decisions?

    Extremely                                                          Not
       Useful   1       2       3       4       5       6       7   Useful

7. Below are several items of additional information which could be but were not provided. Please indicate which of the additional items would be necessary to allow you to make an informed decision regarding the company's request for a loan.

a. Budgets and projected financial statements.

    Absolutely                                                         Not
      Essential  1      2       3       4       5       6       7   Necessary

b. Extensive interviews with owners and corporate officers.

    Absolutely                                                         Not
      Essential  1      2       3       4       5       6       7   Necessary

c. Personal financial statements from owners and corporate officers.

Absolutely                                          Not
Essential 1      2      3      4      5      6      7   Necessary

d. Credit reports from trade creditors.

Absolutely                                          Not
Essential 1      2      3      4      5      6      7   Necessary

e. Credit reports from credit bureaus.

Absolutely                                          Not
Essential 1      2      3      4      5      6      7   Necessary

f. Additional information concerning specific financial statement items. Please specify which items.

    i. _____

Absolutely                                          Not
Essential 1      2      3      4      5      6      7   Necessary

   ii. _____

Absolutely                                          Not
Essential 1      2      3      4      5      6      7   Necessary

  iii. _____

Absolutely                                          Not
Essential 1      2      3      4      5      6      7   Necessary

g. In the spaces below list any other information you would find useful in making your decision and indicate how useful the information would be.

   i. _____

Absolutely                                                    Not
Essential  1      2      3      4      5      6      7    Necessary

  ii. _____

Absolutely                                                  N o t
Essential  1      2      3      4      5      6      7    Necessary

 iii. _____

Absolutely                                                    Not
Essential  1      2      3      4      5      6      7    Necessary


## Background Information

8. How many years have you worked as a bank loan officer? _____

9. What is your current job title? _____

10. How many years have you held this position? _____

11. Do you specialize in evaluating loans for a particular industry?

    If so, what industry? _____

12. What is the size of loan you normally approve? _____

13. What is your educational background? (Circle one)
    a. High school
    b. Some college
    c. Bachelors degree
    d. Some graduate work beyond bachelors degree
    e. Masters degree
    f. Graduate work beyond a masters degree

14. What is the approximate size of your bank in terms of assets? (Circle one)
    a. Under $25 million
    b. $25 to $50 million
    c. $50 to $100 million
    d. $100 to $500 million
    e. $500 million to $1 billion
    f. Over $1 billion

15. What is your home state? _____

THANK YOU FOR YOUR PARTICIPATION IN THIS STUDY

# APPENDIX I
# LETTER TO ABA STUDENTS

October 23, 1988

Dear National Commercial Lending School Students:

We need your help in determining what accounting information is used by lending officers in a short-term commercial lending decision.

An experiment which requires you to review the financial statements and accountants' report of a privately owned corporation and make a lending decision based on that review will be used. The experiment will take approximately 15-20 minutes. Your participation in the experiment is voluntary. However, your participation will provide a valuable service to both the accounting profession and the banking profession. The results of the experiment will be helpful to the accounting profession in determining what information should be provided in financial statements. The results will be helpful to the banking profession in evaluating what information is used in the lending decision and in aiding future training and development.

For your convenience, Greg Bushong will be available in either the Sooner House or the Forum Building to assist you in completing the experiment. Please come by at your convenience to complete the experiment. All responses to the questionnaire are confidential and will be used only in combination with those of other participants.

Your participation is important and will aid us in completing this experiment. Thank you very much for your help.

Sincerely,


Bart P. Hartman, DBA
Professor of Accounting
Louisiana State University


Greg Bushong, CPA
Research Director
Louisiana State University

# APPENDIX J
# LETTER TO GSBS STUDENTS

November 23, 1988


Inside address



Dear Mr. or Mrs.

I need your help in determining what accounting information is relevant in a short-term commercial lending decision.

I am enclosing an experiment which requires you to (1) review the financial statements and accountants' report of a privately owned corporation and (2) make a lending decision based on that review. The experiment will take approximately 15-20 minutes. Your participation will provide a valuable service to me and to both the banking profession and the accounting profession in evaluating what information is used in the lending decision and in aiding future training and development. The results of the experiment will help the accounting profession determine what information should be provided in financial statements.

Please complete the experiment and return it to me in the enclosed envelope by December 9, 1988. All responses to the questionnaire are confidential and will be used only in combination with those of other participants.

Your participation in this experiment is extremely important. Thank you very much for your help. I really appreciate it.

Sincerely,


William F. Staats, Ph.D.
Professor of Banking
Louisiana State University

# APPENDIX K
# REMINDER POST CARD

Dear Mr. or Ms.:

Last week, I mailed you a questionnaire requiring you to make a line of credit decision for a privately held corporation.

If you have already returned the questionnaire, please accept my sincere thanks. If not, please complete and return it today. It is extremely important that your response be included in the study. I sincerely appreciate your help.

Sincerely,

William F. Staats, Ph.D.
Professor of Banking
Louisiana State University

# BIBLIOGRAPHY

Abdel-khalik, A. Rashad, William A. Collins, David P.Shields, Douglas H. Snowball, Ray G. Stephens,and John H. Wragge. *Financial Reporting by Private Companies: Analysis and Diagnosis*. Stamford, CT: Financial Accounting Standards Board, 1983.

Accounting Principles Board. *APB Statement No. 4*, "Basic Concepts and Accounting Principles Underlying Financial Statements of Business Enterprises." New York: American Institute of Certified Public Accountants, 1970.

American Institute of Certified Public Accountants. *Report of the Committee on Generally Accepted Accounting Principles for Smaller and/or Closely Held Businesses*. New York: American Institute of Certified Public Accountants, 1976.

------. *Report of the Special Committee on Small and Medium Sized Firms*. New York: American Institute of Certified Public Accountants, 1980.

------. *Tentative Conclusions and Recommendations of the Special Committee on Accounting Standards Overload*. New York: American Institute of Certified Public Accountants, 1981.

------. *Report of the Special Committee on Accounting Standards Overload*. New York: American Institute of Certified Public Accountants, 1983.

------. *Statement on Auditing Standards No. 58*, "Reports on Audited Financial Statements." New York: American Institute of Certified Public Accountants, 1988.

------. "FASB Issues Statement and Two Technical Bulletins." *The CPA Letter.* 69 (16 January 1989a): 1

------. "FASB Issues Statement; Exposure Draft." *The CPA Letter. 69* (20 February 1989b): 3.

Baker, William Maurice. "The Effects of Accounting Reports on Loan Officers: An Experiment." Ph.D. diss., Virginia Polytechnic Institute and State University, 1987.

Benjamin, James J. and Keith G. Stanga. "Differences in Disclosure Needs of Major Users of Financial Statements." *Accounting and Business Research* 8 (Summer 1977): 187-192.

Benson, Vaughn L. "A Study of the Usefulness of Selected GAAP Basis Accounting Information and its Actual Use in the Small Private Company Loan Decision Process." Ph.D. diss., University of Nebraska-Lincoln, 1985.

Box, G. E. P. and D. R. Cox. "An Analysis of Transformations." *Journal of the Royal Statistical Society* 26 (Series B, 1964): 211-252.

Campbell Jane E. "An Application of Protocol Analysis to the 'Little GAAP' Controversy." *Accounting Organizations and Society* 9 (1984): 329-342.

Casey, Cornelius J. Jr. "Variation in Accounting Information Load: The Effect on Loan Officers' Predictions of Bankruptcy." *The Accounting Review* 55 (January 1980): 36-49.

Conover, W.J. *Practical Nonparametric Statistics.* 2d ed., New York: John Wiley & Sons, 1980.

Cook, Thomas D. and Donald T. Campbell. *Quasi-Experimentation Design & Analysis Issues for Field Settings.* Chicago: Rand McNally College Publishing Company, 1979.

Financial Accounting Standards Board. *Statement of Financial Accounting Standards No. 21*, "Suspension of the Reporting of Earnings per Share and Segment Information by Nonpublic Enterprises." Stamford, CT: Financial Accounting Standards Board. 1978a.

------. *Statement of Financial Accounting Concepts No. 1*, "Objectives of Financial Reporting by Business Enterprises." Stamford, CT: Financial Accounting Standards Board. 1978b.

------. *Statement of Financial Accounting Concepts No. 2*, "Qualitative Characteristics of Accounting Information." Stamford, CT: Financial Accounting Standards Board. 1980.

------. *Invitation to Comment, Financial Reporting by Private and Small Public Companies*. Stamford, CT: Financial Accounting Standards Board. 1981.

------. *Financial Reporting by Privately Owned Companies: Summary of Responses to FASB Invitation to Comment*. Stamford, CT: Financial Accounting Standards Board. 1983.

------. *Statement of Financial Accounting Standards No. 79*, "Elimination of Certain Disclosures for Business Combinations by Non public Enterprises." Stamford, CT: Financial Accounting Standards Board. 1984.

------. *Statement of Financial Accounting Standards No. 95*. "Statement of Cash Flows." Stamford, CT: Financial Accounting Standards Board. 1987a.

------. *Statement of Financial Accounting Standards No. 96*, "Accounting for Income Taxes." Stamford, CT: Financial Accounting Standards Board. 1987b.

------. *Statement of Financial Accounting Standards No. 109*, "Accounting for Income Taxes." Stamford, CT: Financial Accounting Standards Board. 1992.

Hiltebeitel, Kenneth Merrill. "The Accounting Standards Overload Issue: An Empirical Test of the Effect of Four Selected Financial Accounting Standards on the Lending Decisions of Bankers." Ph.D. diss., Drexel University, 1985.

Internal Revenue Service. *Statistics of Income Bulletin*, Summer 1987. Washington, D.C.: U.S. Government Printing Office, 1987.

Isaac, Stephen, and William B. Michael. *Handbook in Research and Evaluation*. San Diego, CA: Edits Publishers, 1981.

Johnson, Douglas A., Kurt Pany, and Richard White. "Audit Reports and the Loan Decision: Actions and Perceptions." *Auditing: A Journal of Practice & Theory* 2 (Spring 1983): 38-51.

Johnson, Richard A., and Dean W. Wichern. Applied Multivariate Statistical Analysis. Englewood Cliffs, NJ: Prentice-Hall, Inc., 1982.

Kirk, Roger. *Experimental Design: Procedures for the Behavioral Sciences*. Monterey, CA: Brooks/Cole Publishing Company, 1982.

Knutson, Dennis L. and Henry Wichmann. "GAAP Disclosures: Problem for Small Business?" *Journal of Small Business Management* 22 (January 1984): 38-46.

Lin, Pao-chuan. "Information Acquisition and Decision Making in Creditors' Decision Environment." Ph.D. diss., Louisiana State University and Agricultural and Mechanical College, 1988.

Miller, Jeffrey Reed. "An Experimental Research Study on the Effects of the Type of Accounting Service on a Bank Lending Decision for Nonpublic Businesses." Ph.D. diss., Louisiana State University and Agricultural and Mechanical College, 1985.

Nair, R. D. and Larry E. Rittenberg. "Professional Notes--Privately Held Businesses is There a Standards Overload?" *Journal of Accountancy* 158 (February 1983): 82-96.

Neter, John, William Wasserman, and Michael H. Kutner. *Applied Linear Statistical Models*. Homewood, IL: Richard D. Irwin, Inc., 1985.

Nunnally, Jum C. *Psychometric Theory*. 2d ed. New York: McGraw-Hill Book Company, 1978.

Pfaffenberger, Roger C., and James H. Patterson. *Statistical Methods for Business and Economics*. Homewood, IL: Richard D. Irwin, Inc., 1977.

Stanga, Keith G. and Mikel G. Tiller. "Needs of Loan Officers for Accounting Information from Large Versus Small Companies." *Accounting and Business Research* 14 (Winter 1983): 63-70.

Swain, Frank S. "Reducing Domestic Barriers to a Strong Economy: A Small Business Agenda." *Journal of Accountancy* 163 (June 1987): 110-116.

U.S. Small Business Administration. *The State of Small Business: A Report of the President*. Washington, D.C.: U.S. Government Printing Office, 1986.

------. *The State of Small Business: A Report of the President*. Washington, D.C.: U.S. Government Printing Office, 1988.

Weston, J. Fred, and Eugene F. Brigham. *Essentials of Managerial Finance* 3d ed., Hinsdale, IL: The Dryden Press, 1974.

Williams, Lowell Kim. "Accounting Standards Overload: A Descriptive Model for Evaluating Perceptions of Accounting Standards." Ph.D. diss., University of Kentucky, 1987.

Winer, B. J., *Statistical Principles in Experimental Design*. New York: McGraw-Hill Book Company, 1971.

# INDEX